Mansions and mud houses

THE STORY OF THE PENN & TYLERS GREEN CONSERVATION AREA

Miles Green

WITH ARCHITECTURAL DETAIL BY
Jo Tiddy

AND PHOTOGRAPHS BY
Eddie Morton and Jo Tiddy

Published by the Penn & Tylers Green Residents Society

© Miles Green 2007

A catalogue record for this book is available from the British Library

ISBN 978-0-9555798

Typesetting and printing by Turville Printing Services,
Unit 2, 67 Verney Avenue, High Wycombe, Bucks HP12 3ND

Visit of Queen Elizabeth to St Margaret's Parish Room in July 1941 to inspect   *(Pat Cuthbert)*
the W.I.'s jam making activities. She is accompanied by Mrs Nora Cuthbert

Photographs – There are a very few copies of old archive photographs, but almost all are originals either by **Eddie Morton, LRPS**, or by **Jo Tiddy**. They are marked (*EM*) or (*JT*) or accordingly.

Space and cost regrettably dictate that inclusion of photographs of newer houses, however attractive, are limited to those illustrating a particular type or having a special interest.

Cover photographs

Front - *Clockwise from the top*:
The Knoll, Pauls Hill, from the south showing the belvedere (*EM*)
Rayners' clock tower (*EM*)
St Anthony's Cottage on Tylers Green Common (*EM*)

Back - *From the top*:
Caricature of Gladstone in a fool's cap with a rat's body removed from the roof of Rayners and put on
    the ridge of The Elms on Elm Road (*EM*)
Watercroft, Church Road (Penn) (*EM*)
Tyler End, Church Road (West), (*JT*)
Dell Cottage, Church Road (West) (*EM*)

Acknowledgements

Nearly 30 years of my fascination with the history of Penn & Tylers Green are distilled in these pages, but the catalyst for bringing them all together has been the formal appraisal of the Conservation Area by the two district councils under the control of Jo Tiddy, Heritage Officer for Wycombe District Council. Our collaboration has been very fruitful and she has produced the three marvellous maps of the Conservation Area to be found on the centre pages and inside the front and back covers. She has also taken many of the 200 photographs and provided most of the architectural detail. It was intended that we should be joint authors, but she has decided that she must move on to other tasks. Nonetheless, I must make it clear that the book would probably not have been written at all, and would certainly not be in its present form, without her invaluable input.

I owe much to the ever-helpful Records Office at Aylesbury for access to documents and copies of maps, as well as to many other libraries and depositories, but I started from the recollections of elderly locals, many of whom are no longer with us. I think of the videos made with Brian Cullip: of Edith White (born 1894), who remembered walking to Old Beaconsfield long before the railway and New Beaconsfield arrived in 1906; of Lilian Clarke (born 1897), who was a postwoman from 1916-22 when the mail came up from Wycombe in a pony and cart; of Evelyn Clark (born 1904), whose father was bailiff to both Earl Howe and Sir Philip Rose and with whom, 25 years ago, I wrote my first little book on local history; of Betty Jollye, whose husband commanded the Home Guard and whose mother greeted the Queen Mother on her visit in 1940.

I also think of; John Broadbent, an architect and former Chairman of the Penn & Tylers Green Society, who worked on many local houses; Pat Cuthbert with her long memories of living on the common and on Paul's Hill; Lady Rose, the widow of the third Sir Philip, who gave me unrestricted access to her family archive; Geoffrey Perfect, whose family built many of our houses; Peter Barnes, who lived on the Back Common almost all his life; Fred Payne, a farmer's boy long before tractors; and many others, all who made their unique contributions.

Then there is Harold Wheeler, now 101, who started life as a grocer's delivery boy in 1915; Walter Carden, now 96, who opened the first garage in Penn at The Crown in 1931, later moving to opposite Slades Garage. David Wooster, now 93, from Penbury Farm, who ran a poultry farm and local dairy. All have impressively accurate recall of their early years.

More immediately, I must thank: Eddie Morton, who not only took photographs of many of the houses and all the maps, but copied and enhanced them and put more than 200 on discs in the order demanded by the text; Bob and Jean Rollason, who have made meticulous and widespread corrections to syntax and punctuation, given expert guidance on the presentation and layout, and taken on the considerable task of preparing the index; and my wife, Iva, whose constant support has enabled me to spend an inordinate amount of time on my researches. I am also grateful to the many house-holders over the years who have allowed visits and the copying of deeds as well as photographs of their houses.

The text is as accurate as I can make it, but work of this kind will inevitably contain many errors and omissions. Any corrections or additions will be welcomed and incorporated in future editions.

Finally, I gladly pay tribute to the patience and skill of Annette and Stuart Hester of Turville Printing Services, who have married text and photographs so effectively.

Explanation of designations
map (inside front cover)

Sub-areas. In order to make such an extensive and varied Conservation Area easier to deal with, it has been divided into five Areas, which largely reflect their different historical development.

A walking route. The buildings are discussed and illustrated in Area order, roughly as you see them if you start around Penn Church and walk down to Potters Cross; then go back to circle first the Front Common, roughly clockwise starting along School Road; then the Back Common, in five further parts, roughly anti-clockwise starting along Rays Lane from the Village Hall end; finishing with Church Road (East) and back to St Margaret's Church and along Church Road (West).

Listed Buildings are indicated in the text by ** and Locally Listed or of significant interest, by*.

Contents

Historical Maps

Introduction

Conservation Areas are areas of special architectural or historic interest, which are considered worthy of preservation or enhancement. At first, Penn and Tylers Green had two separate Conservation Areas, both designated by Buckinghamshire County Council in 1970. The present combined Conservation Area for the two villages was achieved by a series of extensions: in 1981 (by the addition of the Back Common), 1986 (Rayners house and grounds) and 1992 (the top end of Beacon Hill).

The combined Conservation Area is large and very varied, encompassing an area of about 85 acres (34 hectares) with some 329 properties of which 50 are Listed Buildings. There are also Locally Listed and many unlisted buildings, particularly vernacular cottages, which contribute to the special character of the Conservation Area. *The Designations Map* shows the boundaries of the Conservation Area and names all the Listed and Locally Listed buildings. Unlisted buildings often also play an important role and although they are not individually identified on the map many are of considerable interest.

It is an unusual Conservation Area, due in part to the important role that the commons and open spaces within it play in its overall character and to the very different historical development of its component parts, which can still be read from the present day layout. It also, unusually, crosses District Council boundaries: Penn is in the Chiltern District Council area, Tylers Green in that of Wycombe District Council. This presents its own challenges.

Penn is the more rural settlement, lying within the Green Belt and the Area of Outstanding Natural Beauty. There are some 16th and 17th-century buildings close to the 12th-century church, and the far-reaching countryside views from the ridge top of Church Road hasve always attracted prosperous residents. As a result, there are some fine, substantial houses from the 17th to 19th-century houses on large plots aligned to the road; they are the main reason for . John Betjeman's description of Penn as the 'Chelsea of the Chilterns.'

Tylers Green developed when the growth of the chair-making industry in High Wycombe, from c.1800, led to large scale encroachments on the common. Pockets of small vernacular dwellings were built, clustered in and around clay pits, facing on to the open expanses of common. The new settlement took its name from the hamlet on the Penn side of the common. This was called Tyler End because it was on the edge of the common where the medieval Penn tilers had dug their clay.

Road and place names

In order to distinguish clearly between different areas, the following nomenclature has been adopted throughout:

Church Road (Penn) - from the Crown to the entrance to Rayners (Penn School)
Lane End - the earlier name for the area around the top end of Beacon Hill
Tyler End - the earlier name for the part of Penn that is on Elm Road
Church Road (East) - from St Margaret's Parish Rooms, past the Village Hall, to Elm Road
Church Road (West) - from St Margaret's Church, past the Horse & Jockey to Barnes Corner

Historical development

There are six key episodes that have helped create the layout of the present day settlement. In chronological order:

1) *Penn Church* - The foundation of the late 12th-century church at Penn, and the growth of the early settlement core around it and along the ridge top.
2) *Medieval tilers* - The development of the 14th-century tile industry, as a result of which settlement extended up to the edge of the commons of Tyler End Green where the raw material for the industry was readily available, thus creating a secondary core of settlement. This area included the nucleus around the former blacksmith's at the top of Beacon Hill, and the shops and buildings at the southern end of Elm Road.
3) *Tylers Green House (the mansion)* - The 18th-century owners of a mansion over-looking the Front Common near Widmer Pond obtained agreement from the lords of the manor on both sides of the parish boundary to create a park in front of their house by planting trees. It was only the presence of the mansion and its trees that prevented 19th-century encroachment on that part of the common and so has left us with the open Front Common we see today.
4) *Snatch-holders and mud houses* - Piecemeal illegal encroachments on the edge of the common on the Penn side grew during the 18th-century as a result of increasing population pressure; but it was not until c.1800 that the sudden growth of the chair industry in High Wycombe led first to enclosure and then to building on the Tylers Green side of the common. 'Small encroachments …on which mud house were afterwards built…gradually giving place to buildings of a more substantial character.'
5) *Sir Philip Rose of Rayners* - The arrival of Philip Rose and the building of Rayners in 1847 brought fundamental changes. He became the

Penn war memorial & churchyard (EM)

de-facto squire of Tylers Green, employed many of the inhabitants, built St Margaret's Church and owned or built many other buildings, mostly concentrated on the south side of School Road and Church Road (West), i.e. not on the common and so with a more formal layout and 'politer' architectural styles.

6) *'Beaconsfield for Penn' railway station* - The opening of the railway to Marylebone in 1906 encouraged London commuters and coincided with the financial need for the Penn Estate to sell land for building. The whole nature of what had been relatively isolated rural communities was rapidly altered.

The Historical Development Map (centre pages) illustrates the following eight identifiably different components of the Conservation Area which have resulted from this history:

1) The earliest village core of Penn around the 12th-century church.
2) Higher-status residential ribbon development, 17th to 19th-century, along the south side of Church Road towards Beacon Hill on usually large, irregularly spaced plots.
3) Opposite the top of Beacon Hill where the gaps between the few older buildings have been filled in by post-1906 railway development, on long, thin rectangular plots, to join Penn with Tylers Green.
4) The largely 18th and 19th-century shopping area in Elm Road.
5) Buildings associated with the Penn Estate, many of which are on land on which once stood the late medieval mansion that finally became Edmund Burke's school for French émigré boys from 1796 to 1820.
6) The open Front Common around Widmer Pond and the formerly open but now heavily wooded Back Common: here the placing of the tracks and the cottages, resulting from 19th-century encroachments, was dictated by large clay pits. Dwellings are on random-size plots with no consistent orientation.
7) The southern edge of School Road and Church Road (West) which has never been common land and so has earlier and higher-status houses and public buildings mainly associated directly or indirectly with Rayners.
8) The Victorian estate of Rayners, now Penn School, which lies behind high walls within well-wooded and extensive grounds.

1761 Rocque Map - the earliest local map with useful detail

View from Penn church tower (JT)

Area 1: Penn Church

This area has grown up around the late 12th-century church and forms a small traditional village centre. It has a grand house next to the church (The Knoll), which belonged to the manorial family, a former vicarage, a small green (where the stocks used to be) with a war memorial, a former school (Penn Church Hall), a 16th-century pub (The Crown), a Parish Room from where the Vestry administered the parish, and a cluster of old cottages. Most of the buildings are Listed and later refronting often conceals older 17th-century timber-framed buildings. Ribbon development has been encouraged by the abundant ground water along the ridge top towards Tylers Green, and to a lesser extent down Paul's Hill. No shops survive.

Entrance to Penn Church (EM)

Many of the houses along Church Road, Penn, are quite grand with a distinct architectural style and large gardens, taking best advantage of the views that reach as far as Windsor Castle. There are several late 17th-century houses, classed as 'Large Vernacular' - The Knoll, Stonehouse, Pewsey Cottage and Troutwells - and some fine stuccoed Georgian buildings – the Old Vicarage, Southview, and Watercroft. The Methodist Chapel and the Old Reading Room are also significant. The Long Pond plays a decorative role on the roadside and there are some important views to the north towards Puttenham Place. Hedges have occasionally been replaced by high brick walls which can screen the buildings from view, to the detriment of their character.

Penn Church from the main road (JT)

*Penn Church (Holy Trinity)*** is by far the oldest building in the Conservation Area. The church provides the focal point for the village, sitting low at the centre of the almost rectangular one-acre churchyard, which has many fine trees and is surrounded by low late-Victorian flint walls. A graveyard extension to the south, designed by Sir Edward Maufe and completed in 1978, is in a former garden enclosed by an old wall built by the vicar in 1734.

John Betjeman, who knew the village quite well, observed in 1948 that 'within and without, the church has the charm of old water-colours'. Its particular charm is that it is not of any defined period, but is a medley of styles that reflects the changing beliefs and fashions of generations of churchgoers for over eight centuries. The original simple barn-like structure has been transformed into what we see today. The nave is late 12th-century (also the font, consecration crosses and stone tomb), the south aisle and low tower are early 14th-century with the chancel and Lady Chapel largely rebuilt in brick in the 1730s. The clerestory and the fine queen-post roof with arcading were added in c.1400. The nave is built of flint, with clunch and tiles incorporated into parts of the quoins, buttresses and porch. All the exterior roughcast was removed in 1952 to reveal the flint-work and stone.

Penn Church from the south (EM)

The 'Penn Doom', one of only five surviving wooden tympanums in the country, is a 12-foot wide painting of the 'Last Judgement' on oak panels and hangs above the chancel arch. It has twice been on display in the Victoria & Albert Museum in London. There is also an attractive arrangement of 14th-century Penn floor tiles that were set into the floor of the Lady Chapel as part of a millennium project and a fine collection of Tudor and Stuart brasses of the Penn family. There is a well-preserved example of Queen Anne's arms. Six grandchildren of William Penn the Quaker, founder of Pennsylvania, are buried in a large family vault under the centre of the nave. Heraldic shields on the roof corbels portray eight centuries of English history. There is a particularly fine collection of 18th and early 19th-century wall monuments, mainly to the Curzons and Howes.

15th-century Penn Doom (V&A)

The earliest marked grave in the churchyard is of William Penn, the lord of the manor (no relation to William Penn the Quaker), who died in 1693. There are many well-known names, and two are notorious: Donald Maclean who defected to Russia in 1951 and David Blakeley who was shot in 1955 by Ruth Ellis, the last woman to be hanged in England.

Nameplate on a coffin in the Penn family vault (Brian Cullip)

The Home Guard. In the Second World War, for three and a half years, the church tower was an observation post for the Home Guard's nightly watch from a wooden sentry box erected on the roof. The book recording their duty in four-hour shifts starts on 29 June 1940, a few weeks after Dunkirk and Churchill's uplifting 'This was their finest hour' speech. A German invasion was thought to be imminent and over a million men enrolled in the Home Guard, although at first they only had shot guns. Road signs were removed, place names painted out and metal railings and gates (including the Rayners and Yonder Lodge main gates) and pots and pans were sent off to make ships, tanks and planes. The book is at its busiest during the Battle of Britain from July to September 1940, when distant searchlights, fires, bombs and aircraft are reported; but the closest enemy aircraft or bombs came to the tower was two or three miles away, and 'nothing to report' often records what must have been a long night. It used to be claimed that 12 counties could be viewed from the top of the tower, and a former Home Guard remembered that it was said that with the aid of binoculars one could see the outskirts of Portsmouth. They could certainly see Windsor Castle, Ascot racecourse, Northolt airport and the outskirts of London, as well as American planes landing at Brackley in Northampton, some 40 miles away.

Home Guard outside Slades Garage, Beacon Hill (Betty Jollye)

Home Guard outside The Crown (Betty Jollye)

Pat Cuthbert remembered the exhilaration of walking up Paul's Hill in the evening of the day the war ended, hearing the church bells pealing away for the first time that she remembered since the fall of France in 1940 (although they were rung after the victory at Alamein in 1942), and seeing the streams of light from open doors and windows celebrating the end of the blackout. While church bells could be tolled during the war, a peal was reserved for warning of enemy invasion.

Village Green. The buildings around the small green and down Paul's Hill are the oldest in the Conservation Area. The village stocks used to stand on this green beneath two very old elm trees, the second of which finally collapsed in 2001. The *War Memorial* to those who died in the First World War was put up in 1922 and dedicated by Field

Small village green at Penn including the whitebeam planted in 1997 to replace the last stock elm (EM)

The two stock elms on the green, now gone (Mrs Everett)

The Crown (EM)

The oldest part of the Crown (JT)

Church & Crown Cottage (EM)

Paul's Hill cottages (EM)

Marshal Sir William Robertson. The names of those killed in the Second World War were added after 1945. The *red telephone box*** on the green was Listed in 1989. Made of cast iron, it is a type K6, designed by Sir Giles Gilbert Scott in 1935.

The Crown** lies across the road to the north east of the churchyard, and is very probably one of the two alehouses recorded in Penn in 1577. It is one of the four public houses still open in the Conservation Area. The oldest part of the building is 16th-century (note that its chimney is built well outside the line of the wall), with late 18th and 20th-century (1934) additions. The original part is of red and grey brick with band courses, under an old tile roof. Later wings and porch are harmonious. The Crown stands right at the edge of the village where Witheridge (formerly Witherage) Lane winds up from Beaconsfield and the ancient pub plays an important part in the street-scene around the small green and war memorial opposite. It was an inn with five bedrooms and Penn Estate rent suppers and large shooting parties were hosted there. During the Second World War it was the 'local' for the Home Guard. It was owned by the Penn Estate with the Darvill family as landlords for over a century from the 1750s and the Garlands from 1864 until 1929 when the inn was sold.

Crown Cottage**, opposite the Crown, is a good example of a timber-framed 16th/17th-century cottage with brick infill panels. Holy Trinity's verger lived there for many years. Two cottages were put into one in 1999.

Paul's Hill has an important and picturesque grouping of 16th to 18th-century Listed cottages which sit hard on the roadside. *Stone Cottage*** and *Nos 1-3 Church Cottages*** are of flint with brick dressings, concealing earlier timber-framing. Their old tile roof is enlivened by many chimneys, including a particularly fine example of triple-shafted brick. *Nos 5 and 6 Church Cottages*** are 17th-century, one and a half storeys, with dormers under a tile roof, and again chimney stacks that add to their character.

No 4, The *Parish Room***, is of particular interest. It was refronted in brick with a hipped roof, probably c.1730s, when converting a 16th-century timber-framed house built at right angles to the road. This was in order to provide a room to be used by the Vestry for poor relief administration. It seems to have been part of far-reaching changes when Sir Nathaniel Curzon inherited the manor from Roger Penn and was making radical alterations to the church, rebuilding the chancel, raising the roof and adding a vestry. The Parish Pay Room, as it was called, was where the Vestry administered the parish. This included setting and collecting the poor rate and other taxes four times a year, and paying out monthly relief to the poor, who could be as many as a quarter of the parish after a bad harvest. Cottages for the poor were built by 1744, some of them on Beacon Hill.

The Parish Room was also used as a lace school and a Sunday school. There was apparently a small shop and a pub at the back. The first election of a Parish Council took place there in 1894 and it was used more recently for occasional gaslit meetings of the Parish Council meetings until conversion in 2002 to an office. Parish records back to

1804 and beyond were found in a locked safe in 1995. There is a big porch to one side, good brick hood moulds to the ground floor and 19th-century casement windows.

The former Parish Room from the graveyard (JT)

Hatchits, which lies behind the two groups of Church Cottages, is a large elaborately-thatched house. It was the winning design of the Ideal Home Exhibition in 1927, but it was a good deal smaller and had a tiled roof when it was first built. The first owner was Mrs Nora Cuthbert, the war-widowed mother of the late Betty Jollye and Pat Cuthbert, and she had the house enlarged and thatched in c.1930. Mrs Cuthbert's son-in-law, Lt S.A.Jollye, purchased the house in 1939. He was in charge of the Home Guard in the Second World War; his wife was the Quartermaster and Hatchits was their HQ with the entrance hall as their armoury and Mills bombs stored in the garage. The fifth Earl Howe lived there from 1953 to 1960. The house takes its name from Hatchetts Mead, the name of the former field in which it stands. It is not currently in the Conservation Area, but should be included.

Paul's Hill Cottages (EM)

*The Knoll*** is a fine house to the rear of the churchyard, built in 1671 for the newly married Nathaniel Curzon and his wife Sarah Penn. It is a fine example of a small country house of an intermediate stage of housebuilding with external brick walls supporting the roof, but with the whole interior supported by a heavy oak frame. It is of red brick with a hipped tiled roof and it retains original casement windows on the north side with later sashes elsewhere. There is a tiled turret or belvedere in the roof on the south side from which, as local legend has it, Queen Anne sat watching her children play on the lawn at Windsor. Apart from the fact that there is a marvellous view and you can see Windsor on a good day, there is no evidence for this story. A far more likely possibility is that the belvedere was originally built as an observatory. The Rev. Benjamin Anderson (1733-1812) lived in the house for some years before he became vicar in 1808. He was a friend of Edmund Burke who described him in letters in 1795 to the then Home Secretary and Secretary at War, as 'a Clergyman at Penn…of Learning & merit… whose Observatory and Experimental apparatus I wished much to shew you'. (Walter Carden of White Cottage, Church Road (Penn) is a great-great-great-grandson of the Rev. Anderson).

Hatchits (EM)

Mrs Frances Knollis, wife of the vicar from 1823-60 lived in The Knoll for 20 years after her husband died. Sir George Robertson lived there from 1927 to 1939. He was a brilliant classical scholar who threw the discus for England in the first Olympic Games, after first composing and then reciting a Greek ode. The Countess Howe, the divorced first wife of the fifth Earl, moved to The Knoll in 1945, and was followed by her son, Viscount Curzon, who lived there until he moved back into Penn House. The house, having been in Curzon hands for nearly three centuries, was sold in 1956. Ernest Saunders, the convicted Chairman of Guinness, was a later owner.

The Knoll (EM)

Penn Church Hall, a former school (EM)

Penn Church Hall (EM)

Penn Church Hall (EM)

Former almshouses, now gone

The Old Vicarage (JT)

The *Church Hall*** lies opposite the church lych-gate. It stands on the site of the Parish Workhouse to which the earliest reference, in 1773, is to the first child to be born there, his father having been transported. It was replaced, in 1839, by a working school for girls, designed by Edward Blore for the first Earl Howe, in memory of his wife whose arms coronet and initials - HGH for Harriet Georgiana Howe - are displayed above the gable window. Edward Blore (1787-1879) was appointed 'special architect' to William IV and hence his connection with Earl Howe, who was Lord Chamberlain to Queen Adelaide. The same architect also carried out various works at Windsor Castle for Queen Victoria and, in 1846, designed the front of Buckingham Palace to complete the quadrangle. Blore specialised in Gothic, Tudor and Elizabethan styles and our hall was built in Tudor style in an imported yellow brick. Boys joined the girls not long after their school at Church Knoll was closed in 1875, and the building was extended, in 1910, to a design by Harrison-Townsend. The school closed in 1949 for lack of pupils.

Penn Mead flats. In 1830 there was a labourers' revolt in the southern counties born of unemployment and poverty. Severe rioting took place in Wycombe Marsh and Loudwater. It can be no coincidence that in 1831 an asylum, 'for the indigent poor of the parish', later to be known as the *Almshouses*, was built on this site close to the church. It was paid for by Earl Howe and John Grove of Watercroft. This historic building was pulled down in 1967 and replaced by *Penn Mead* flats, designed by Sir Hugh Casson. Vehement opposition to this was the reason for the formation of the Penn & Tylers Green Society in 1965.

By far the majority of high-status houses in the Conservation Area are found along the ridge top of Church Road, Penn, many of them Listed. Until the arrival of the railway at Beaconsfield, there were only four houses and the Methodist chapel on the north side of the road between Penn Church and Tylers Green, so the houses on the south side had a glorious view to the north as well as to the south.

*The Old Vicarage*** is a white-painted, stuccoed, early 19th-century Georgian villa in the classical style (with later extensions), with Welsh slate roofs and later extensions. It was built by the Rev. James Knollis, vicar of Penn, at his own expense in 1825. He noted that it had 'Ground floor, 4 rooms, 2 kitchens, 2 pantries; on first floor, 6 bed chambers, 2 dressing rooms and a water closet.' There is supposed to be an underground passage from the cellar to the church which was blocked up 40 or so years ago. The excitement of two visits by King William and Queen Adelaide, in 1833 and 1835, is recorded in two long letters. General Sir Brian Robertson lived there briefly after the Second World War. He was Military Governor and C in C for the British Occupation Zone in Germany from 1947 to 1949, succeeding the then General Montgomery who visited him at the house in 1945. It was General Robertson's father, Field Marshal Sir William Robertson, who had dedicated the Penn War Memorial in 1922. A century after it was built, the Old Vicarage became too expensive for a vicar to run, and was sold in 1925 to Mrs Ralph Heal. She moved in c.1932 to Tithe Cottage, a large new house on the glebeland opposite the Old Vicarage hidden by a hedge and by the slope of the ground, now known as *Penn Court*.

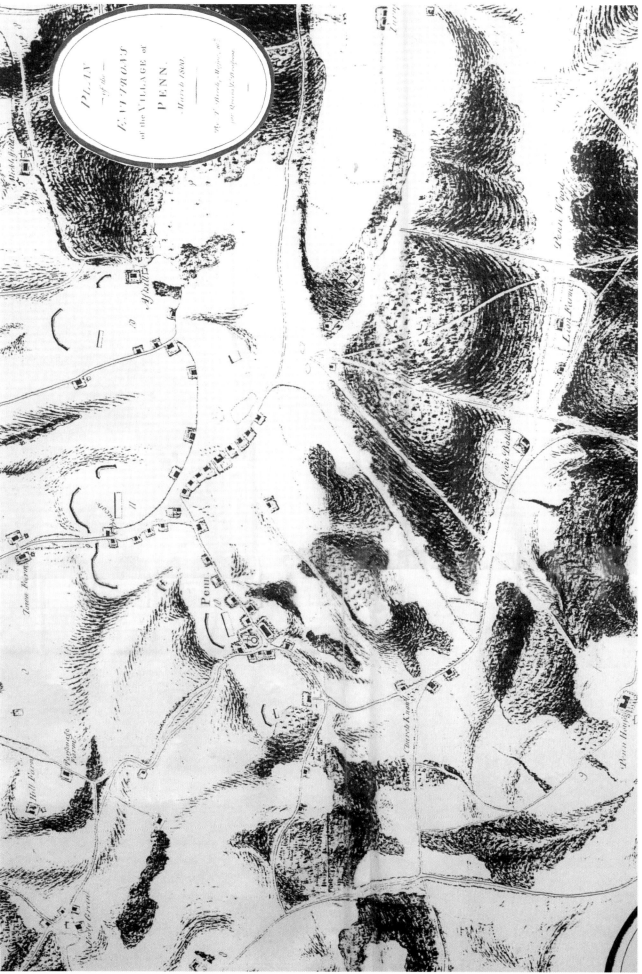

PLAN
— of the —
ENVIRONS of
PENN.
March 1800

By T. Wards, Major, &c.
(or Royal E. Dragoons)

Penn Wood

Lion Farm

Penn Bottom

Town Farm

Penn

Church Farm

Penn House

Hill Farm

1800 Military Map - made by an army officer on horseback using a compass

(The Print Room, The Royal Library, Windsor Castle)

Southview (JT)

Stonehouse Grange (JT)

Long Pond (EM)

Stonehouse (EM)

Southview**, another Georgian villa, is almost hidden behind a high brick wall built in the 1980s in 1987 when the house was largely rebuilt, except for the façade, by an unscrupulous developer. For many years between the wars it was the home of John Widdowson, who succeeded his father as the steward of the Penn Estate. He organised enormous shooting parties, frequently attended by Joachim von Ribbentrop, German ambassador to London 1936 to 1938, who later became Hitler's foreign minister and was and hanged following the Nuremberg trials. John Widdowson ran the estate from his office in the brick and flint cottage in the garden, which has just been pulled down, and used to do his rounds of the estate, which then covered 90% of the parish, on horseback until he was 80.

Stonehouse Grange is a large modern country house set well back from the roadside, built in 1984 in a traditional style in part of the Stonehouse garden. The low brick boundary wall is fronted by *Long Pond* in which a drunken Roundhead soldier in armour is said to have drowned. The parish register records the burial of 'Jas Smith, a souldier', on 18 July 1643.

Stonehouse** is an early 19th-century refacing of an earlier jettied, medieval timber-framed house in which fragments of 17th-century wall painting have been found in a ground floor cupboard. The house belonged to the Grove family from the Middle Ages until 1952. Edmund Grove (1729 -1823) is said to have been a favourite of George III, who greeted him as 'Yeoman Grove' and visited Stonehouse where pewter plates bearing the royal arms were preserved. The story goes that George III, meeting Edmund Grove in the market at Windsor, told him that he had seen him through his new telescope from the Round Tower walking on the Stonehouse lawn wearing a plum coat and eating cherries. In 1860, a stoneware mug inscribed '1737 Geo Grove', full of golden guineas, was found up a chimney. The building has good early casement windows and a bracketed hood over the front door. One bay has blind windows to the ground and upper floors. The steep hipped roof, with rendered stack, is of Welsh slate, a material which is also utilised on some of the roadside brick farm buildings. Veronica Papworth, a well-known fashion writer in her day, lived there from 1953 to 1980. Alexander Shephard, a recent owner, was High Sheriff of the county in 2001/02.

There are a number of adjacent former farm buildings, once part of the Stonehouse Farm. *Grove's Barn*, converted to a house in the 1950s and not Listed, includes a clay-tiled and weather-boarded granary. Elizabeth Taylor, the novelist (see *Penn Cottage* below) lived there before her death in 1975. A *Listed barn*** of three bays with a queen-post roof with lovely timbering is now in the curtilage of Wellbank House. It is an unusual fine example of a late 16th or early 17th-century barn reclad and with a lean-to added on the east in the 18th-century. It is believed that it may have been built in Oxfordshire, and dismantled and moved to Penn in c.1834. *Wellbank House* (formerly Oakmead House) is an extended and impressive 1930s house, built by Frank Perfect, a local builder, perhaps on top of a kiln because tiles similar to those in the church tower were found there. It shares with its neighbours the wonderful view of Windsor Castle and has a permanently running small stream. Stumps Lane, which leads to Stumpwell, the spring which supplied village water until the mains arrived in 1912, runs along one side of the garden.

Former Stonehouse barn, now with Wellbank House (EM)

Wellbank (EM)

*Pewsey Cottage,***formerly Pusey Cottage, is a picturesque late 17th-century house, very probably a former lodge to Puttenham Place. A track to Puttenham still exists opposite, and the building detailing is similar to that of the Old Bank House in Elm Road. The building is of brick with two Dutch gables to the road side, and a further decorative gable facing east on the single-storey range. A brick stringcourse at first floor level adds visually interest to this pretty building. From 1913 to 1937, it was called Ivy Cottage and was a popular tearoom/guest house run by Mrs Pusey for walkers and cyclists. The visitors' book is full of superlatives about the teas and the rural charm of the locality. One thanks her for 'such a ripping rest and feed'. It was never, as popular legend had it, one of Henry VIII's hunting lodges.

Pewsey Cottage (JT)

*Troutwells*** is a subdivided dwelling of some size, late 17th-century, with later projecting wings, now separate houses, *Grove Cottage*** and *Troutwells End***. The oldest part, in the centre, is of red brick with grey headers and with red brick quoins and dressings. The clay-tiled roofs have a modillion cornice and myriad chimneys punctuating the skyline. Sir Courtenay Peregrine Ilbert lived in Troutwells as one house from 1912 into the 1920s. He was a barrister who had been senior legal adviser to the Governor General of India and then Clerk to the House of Commons (1902-21). There is a spring pond in the garden. The house was subdivided c.1950s.

Troutwells (JT)

To the north of the road, there are newer developments. *Penn Ridge* (formerly *Marlins,* the name of the field) built for a Colonel Murray in c.1913, and *Penn Lodge* (c.1953, formerly *Lark Rise*) are both substantial detached houses with a vague Arts and Crafts theme. Penn Ridge has unusual gables. Opposite, *Springfield* is a very recent (2004) replacement of an older house.

Alde House is an adaptation of a house first called *Swiss Cottage* owned and occupied by one of the Grove family in the 1890s and tenanted in 1913 with an acre of land. There was a house on the site by 1851 which was occupied by a fundholder and his wife and a servant. It had been enlarged or rebuilt to its present width by 1875. Harold Wheeler, now 101, remembers that the house, unusually for Penn, already had three stories and a thatched roof which was removed after

Penn Ridge (JT)

Alde House (EM)

Manor House (JT)

Penn Cottage (JT)

a bad fire in about 1917. He and his school friends took time off from school to watch a horsedrawn fire engine from Wycombe with a steam pump dealing with the fire. It had been renamed *Little Hatch* by 1915 and was occupied by Laurence Hall, an architect (Tel. Penn 21). A Lady Orde was living there for much of the 1930s. When it was sold in 1970, with its three stories and eight bedrooms, it was described as 'developed over many years from a period cottage'. The house was opened in 1972 as as a residential home for the elderly of the village by a local group inspired and led by Geoffrey Perfect, son of Frank Perfect the builder, whose family has lived in Penn for many generations.

*Manor House** was once the home of the steward of the small part of Segraves Manor that was in Penn. It was the traditional meeting place of the Segraves Manor Court, although in later years its members then customarily repaired to the Red Lion and held their meetings there. In the 1930s, antiques were sold here and it briefly became a tea garden. It is an 18th-century stuccoed building which has been Victorianised by the insertion of large square bay windows into the front elevation. The architectural detail of the older building can still be glimpsed in the form of the door hood and blind window above. The roof is hipped and of tile. The building is linked visually to the next by a long, high roadside brick wall which encloses the garden of Watercroft.

Penn Cottage**, to the north of the road, is a colour-washed, rendered mid-18th-century cottage, with a symmetrical front elevation, a blind central window, and a hipped tiled roof. A deed of 1735 records a house built that year which, from the description of its location, was very probably this cottage. Daniel Baker granted John Flexman, a tailor, 1,100 square yards on which the cottage stood that had been built the same year, 'together with a water course and fall in and through a meadow called Paviors.' Paviors was to the west and there was a wood called Holmore to the north. It was a carpenter's house and yard (Garland's) in 1851. It was later the home of Elizabeth Taylor, described by Antonia Fraser as 'one of the most underrated novelists of the 20th-century', for most of her married life from the 1940s. She moved down the road to Grove's Barn in the last few years of her life. The adjacent *Hillbrow Cottage* is based on a bungalow built in the former garden of Penn Cottage in 1971.

Watercroft (EM)

Watercroft** was built in about 1815 by John Grove, another member of the Grove family from Stonehouse. A later owner was his nephew, Sir George Grove (1820-1900), the original author of the Dictionary of Music and Musicians, the bible of music lovers. After a visit in 1885, he wrote that 'on either side of the street are some of the most delightful fields in England, and thence you may have unrivalled views'. Arthur Sullivan, who was a close friend and godfather to one of Grove's sons, is variously said to have written 'The Lost Chord', 'Onward Christian Soldiers' and 'Tit Willow' from The Mikado in the former summerhouse at Watercroft. Stumpwell, at the

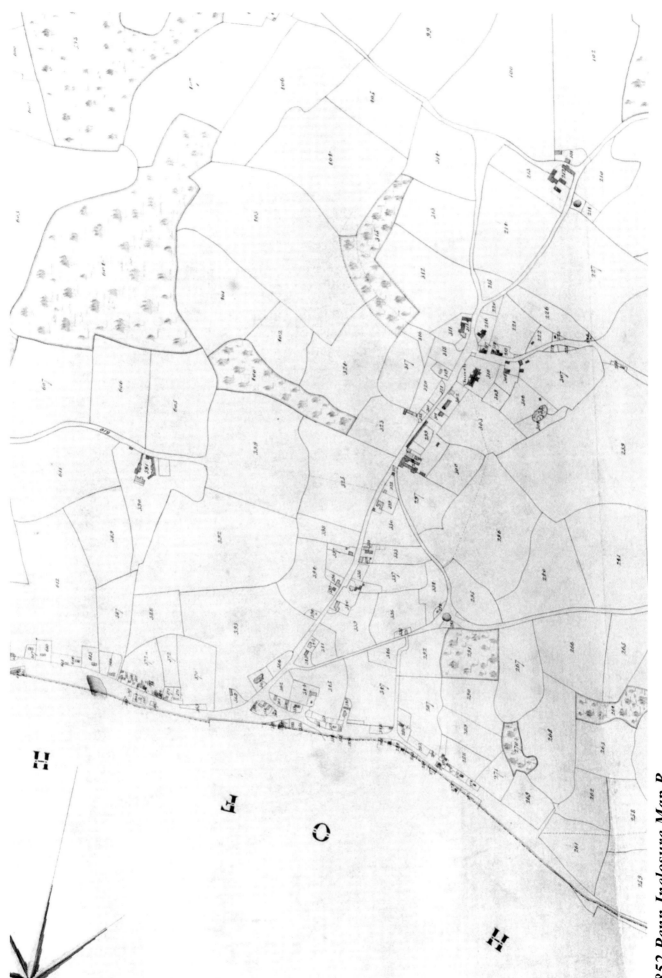

1852 Penn Inclosure Map B

17

Free Methodist Chapel (EM)

Chapel Cottage (JT)

The Chinnery's door hood (EM)

bottom end of the garden, is said to have been a favourite resort of nightingales. The house is aligned side-on to the road; the eastern front, glimpsed above the garden wall, has a superb set of windows on both floors. Their wrought-iron balconies are said to have been made by Napoleonic POWs, whose names were inscribed on the leaded well of the roof, but have been removed by more recent extensions. The building is linked to its former coach house which has a brewery to the rear. An earlier owner remembered that both Churchill and Attlee, when they were Prime Minister, used to drive by en-route from London to Chequers. Sir Barrie Heath, a Battle of Britain Spitfire pilot with a DFC and later group chairman of GKN, lived there from 1965 until his death in 1988. As a sailor, he won the Admiral's Cup for Britain in 1963. Mary Berry, the well-known food writer and TV cook, lives there now.

The *Wesleyan Methodist Chapel,* opposite Watercroft, is not Listed, but dates from 1808 and was the first Free Methodist chapel in the Wycombe area. The original, simple red-brick building at right-angles to the road, is named as 'Providence Chapel' on the 1875 map. In that year, a new chapel of yellow brick was added to the west and the original chapel was converted to a schoolroom and refaced with yellow stocks at the roadside end. The chapel was again extended to the west in 1911 and there have since been further extension to the rear of the original chapel. The 1851 religious census shows that Penn was then a very strongly Methodist parish with 580 villagers attending three services or Sunday school on the census day. This number represented half the parish, more than the 471 who attended Holy Trinity, and must have been a tight squeeze in the first small chapel. The small and probably older *Chapel Cottage** (both are on the 1811 map) next to it, still occupied by the Methodist minister, is of brick with three bays, the westernmost a later addition. It faces directly on to the road.

Beyond the chapel, the road dips, and to the south, *The Chinnery* (formerly *Dell Cottage*) has an untypical new flint wall to the front which does not follow vernacular tradition. It was a pair of workmen's cottages rented shortly before 1911 by Lord Dawson of Penn, George V's doctor, as a country retreat. He converted the cottages to what he described as a 'library with cottage attached'. Lord Dawson was one of the first London-based commuters. The first transatlantic telephone call ever made was in 1927, from Pennsylvania via a temporary cable from Penn Post Office to Lord Dawson. This was in the mistaken belief that, because of his title, he was a descendant of William Penn, the founder of Pennsylvania. The house has since been much altered, although the front elevation retains its sash windows and a particularly graceful door hood. Lord Dawson, who left Penn in 1938, is particularly remembered for his bulletin 'the King's life is moving peacefully towards its close', as George V lay dying. An envious colleague taunted his rival with the disrespectful jingle:

'Lord Dawson of Penn
Has killed many men
So that's why we sing
God save the King'

The Chinnery (formerly Dell Cottage) (JT)

Penn's medieval tilers

There is a documentary reference to a Penn tiler in 1222, and another in 1296 when roof and ridge tiles were sold to a royal household in Berkhamstead. By 1332, there were three tilers in Penn whose combined wealth equalled that of the lord of the Manor. For two or three generations in the 14th-century Penn was home to England's leading floor tilers and Penn floor tiles were far and away the most popular choice for royal palaces and castles, cathedrals, abbeys, churches and manor houses all over London and the south-east. The tilers were working at Windsor Castle for eight years laying more than a quarter of a million tiles. There were nearly 200 different designs, the majority singles, but many 4-tile and a few 9-tile and mosaic patterns. Only one complete floor survives – in the Aerary (treasury) in Windsor Castle - but evidence of tiled floors has been found in 180 different sites in 18 counties as well as in 80 sites in London.

Medieval Penn tiles on the corridor to the Aerary, Windsor Castle (EM)

The 1222 tiler was from Knotty Green and presumably gave the name to Clay Street, but eight of the ten tile designs found on the Aerary floor at Windsor Castle, which were laid in 1355, have also been found in three gardens at the top end of Beacon Hill which all back on to the same deep clay pit. This phase of Penn's tile industry was clearly focussed there. The tilers would have required a blacksmith for their carts, the predecessor, perhaps, of Slades Garage and a water supply, presumably from Pistles Pond. It is also clear from the location of other tile finds (see *Historical Development Map* on centre pages) and the many clay pits on the commons, that at some stage the tilers had their kilns fronting the common all the way from Beacon Hill down to Yonder Lodge. Documented royal orders show that, at their busiest, the tilers were operating at least 15 kilns all working flat out to meet the demand for floor and roof tiles. They completely dominated the parish economy and even changed the name of their part of the parish from Garret Green to Tyler End Green.

Medieval Penn tiles on the floor of the Aerary (EM)

Mosaic of medieval Penn tiles on the floor of the Lady Chapel, Penn Church (EM)

A cab waiting for passengers for Penn at Beaconsfield Station c.1906 (CWPC)

Beaconsfield for Penn railway station

In 1900, a walk from Penn Church to Old Beaconsfield passed only a few farms and cottages. The road was dusty and made up with flints and there were only horse-drawn vehicles. There were about 1,000 people in the whole parish of whom some 600 lived in Penn village. Penn Parish Council had warmly supported a railway station, predicting in all innocence, that 'the Hamlet of Penn including Tylers Green has about 1,500 inhabitants and there are several gentlemen having residences in London who would doubtless use the Beaconsfield station in their journey to and from London'. Little did they realise that the whole nature of the parish was about to change. The railway arrived in 1906, a garage opened in Knotty Green, and Witherage Lane had to be widened. The Penn Estate, which owned most of the parish's 4,000 acres, was to sell over half of them during the next half-century. The population of Penn parish doubled by 1950 and quadrupled by the end of the century with half living in Knotty Green.

An unexpected consequence was to divide Penn and Tylers Green. The second Sir Philip Rose, writing in 1911 about arrangements to celebrate the coronation of George V said 'I think we must recognise that since the last occasion when Coronation festivities were the subject of consideration a great change has taken place in Penn parish. In 1902 Penn, so far as any considerable population is concerned, may be said to have ended near Penn Church. Now there is a considerable population at the other end of the parish, nearer in fact to Beaconsfield than to Tylers Green, and another centre at Knotty Green. It may be therefore that Penn parish, including these new districts, would prefer to work independently as, no doubt, it is well able to do.'

Great Central Railway.

Price £ 5.13.9

ISSUED TO

Mr G. Cuthbert

THIS Ticket is issued upon the special conditions set forth in the Company's Time Table, and on the terms that the holder shall be subject to the same rules and regulations as other passengers.

Available from.... apl 2nd 1906 ....to

30 JUNE 06

This Ticket is not transferable, and must be given up immediately on expiration. Any use of this Ticket after the date of expiry will be an offence under the "Regulation of Railways Act, 1889."

No. 1/1

SAM FAY, General Manager.

The first quarterly season ticket (first class) between Beaconsfield and Marylebone
(Pat Cuthbert – her father's ticket)

Area 2: Lane End

Until after the First World War, all the way along Church Road from the Methodist Chapel to Beacon Hill, there were open fields to the north and only three buildings to the south. The houses around the top end of Beacon Hill were identified in old records as a separate hamlet known as 'Lane End' because it was at the end of Church Lane (the earlier name for Church Road) before it reached the cattle gate across the road near the Rayners entrance, which was referred to as Tyler End Green gate. This separation of hamlets was lost with the arrival of the railway at Beaconsfield.

Little Mead (JT)

The formerly open, north side of the road is now filled by a run of largely unaltered 'cottage style' detached houses. *Oldfields* (1955), opposite Lane House, occupies a plot of one acre, but is excluded from the Conservation Area. *Keld Cottage, Culverley, Little Mead* and *Birnam Cottage* were all built c.1930 by local builders Will and Frank Perfect, who also built *The Vicarage* (formerly *Twichels*) in 1920. The Vicarage was purchased in 2003 for the first Vicar of both Penn and Tylers Green, and was chosen in part because it is midway between the two churches. The houses are all individually designed, but tied together by shared detailing of brickwork and chimneys and a similar plot layout. They exhibit many of the characteristics of the fashionable Arts and Crafts style of the time with sweeping gables, porches, casement windows with leaded lights, applied tile hanging and sprocketed eaves. *The Meadows* (1972) has many of the same attractive features and was built in the garden of Yew Tree House.

The Vicarage (formerly Twichels) (JT)

Lane House, on the south side of the road, is another 'railway' infill. this large house with tile-hung gables, then called Little Shelter, was built not long before 1911 and has since been extended several times. It is set back from the road with some fine mature trees to the front. and a brick wall and hedging screen along the frontage A large clay pit in the front garden was filled in a few years ago.

Lane House (JT)

Stumpwell Cottage (formerly *Stamp Cottage),* is so called because it is next to one of the three lanes leading to the former village water supply at Stampwell or Stumpwell. It has an 18th-century exterior with considerable modern extensions and has some internal indication of heavy timbering. 15th-century pottery sherds have been found in the garden. The 1841 census shows a grocer living there. Harold Wheeler, now aged 101, was a grocer's delivery boy in the 1920s and remembers a coachman by the name of Ernest Buckles living in the cottage who ran a horse-drawn taxi service in a brougham with the passengers in the covered cab and the bowler-hatted driver outside. The widow of the 5th Earl Howe (his third wife) lived in the cottage from 1963 to 1971, and it was considerably extended both then and recently.

Stumpwell Cottage (JT)

Old Reading Room Cottage (EM)

Grasside (JT)

Tamarisk Cottage, modern and timber-clad, is hidden by hedging on the corner of the lane to Stumpwell. *Solveig's Cottage* was built by Geoffrey Perfect in c.1970. *Old Reading Room Cottage* is shown as a boys' and girls' school on the 1875 map, in addition to the school opposite the church. It was built in about 1875 of red brick obtained from the dismantling of from the former boys' school at Church Knoll. It was a school for only a year or so and was then set up by the second Earl Howe as the Penn Institute & Reading Room, a working men's club where tea and coffee replaced beer, and newspapers and magazines were passed on by the gentry. It closed in 1960. It is in an Arts and Crafts style with later windows inserted on a smaller scale. The steep gables to the front and low eaves add interest to the sweeping tiled roof. *Grasside*, adjacent, is an Edwardian villa, with rendered upper floor and applied half-timbering. Large quantities of medieval Penn tile fragments have been found in the back garden, many of which are now set in the new plinth in the Lady Chapel of Penn Church.

Cobblers**, formerly Rose Cottage, on the corner of Church Road and Beacon Hill, is a perfect example of a small Georgian house with a handsome red and grey chequer brick façade to Church Road, under a hipped tiled roof with end stacks. There are fine sash windows, a dummy central window and a decorative trellised door surround. The

Cobblers (JT)

building sits within a corner plot, and on the Beacon Hill side there are brick and flint walls to the side and rear elevations. The garden railings to the front are included in the listing and there is an unusual 'railway' carport at the side. The house was built in 1805, probably by the first owner, Charles Garland, and his father. Both were carpenters. Charles Garland was apparently closely involved in building Penn Street Church for the first Earl Howe in 1849. He was a Methodist, although his uncle, the Rev Benjamin Anderson, was Vicar of Penn from 1808-12 and his grandfather, William Clarke, was steward for the Penn Estate.

Wren Cottage (EM)

Along Beacon Hill there is a huddle of vernacular cottages, mostly 19th-century, generally well-spaced in their random plots and set against a wooded background.

Wren Cottage (pre-1838) is a good example of the upper end of the vernacular architecture scale: the building uses higher quality material, dressings and layout with, like Cobblers opposite, a 'respectable' brick front. The Victorians despised flint work using words like 'wretched' and 'inferior' to describe brick and flint cottages.

Yew Tree Cottage, tucked away within its site, is older, with some timber-framing and is white painted with weatherboarded details. Some of the most interesting Penn tiles have been found in the rear garden.

Pistles Pond (*Cottage*) is an unusually authentic modern copy of an early 19th-century cottage. It was built by John Lunnon in 1990 with close attention to detail, even to varying the size of brick. *Pistles Pond* behind the cottage once belonged to a farm which is recorded in 1332 as Pussulle (probably 'Peas Hill', where the wild pea flower grew). *Well Cottage* and *Rayner's Cottage* back on to Pistles Pond and belonged to the Rayners Estate, but may precede it since there were cottages already there on the 1840 map. *Field House* is the exception to the vernacular style – it is a modern (1990s) house , but of late 19th-century stucco and slate design, in the classical style, set behind the woodland belt. It replaced a house owned by Sir James Helmore, a top civil servant, and Permanent Secretary. The small *Wash Pond*, another of the ponds marking the parish boundary, is right by the roadside. *Beacon Hill Cottage,* an attractive, white-painted vernacular cottage with extensions, marks the end of the Conservation Area on Beacon Hill.

Yew Tree Cottage (EM)

Pistles Pond cottage (JT)

Pistles Pond (EM)

Rayners Cottages before extensions

Field House (JT)

Wash Pond (EM)

Beacon Hill Cottage (EM)

23

Slades Garage (JT)

Walnut Cottage (EM)

Slades Garage was a blacksmith's and was still a smithy, shoeing horses, until the 1930s. It was built in a vaguely Art Deco style, particularly the decorative pilaster effects. The original smithy cottage, *Walnut Cottage*, is a small vernacular building of brick with an unusual and very tall chimney stack to the road elevation and a correspondingly impressive late 18th-century inglenook fireplace inside with additions at the front which have dates of 1840 and 1860 CW inscribed in the brickwork. CW probably refers to Charles Wingrove, born in 1838. William Wingrove appears as a blacksmith in the Posse Comitatus of 1798. The Wingrove family were blacksmiths here well back into the 18th-century and Stephen Wingrove was still the blacksmith in 1883. Walter Evans had taken over by 1887 and was succeeded in his turn by George Slade in about 1915. *Amberley Cottage*, the brick and flint cottage next door, was built by Geoffrey Perfect in the 1960s and replaced an older house in which Mr Peat, one of the gardener's at Rayners, used to live.

Yew Tree House **, on the opposite side of the road, is presumably the one described in the Penn Church register in 1733 as, 'Mr Wm Lee's house in Lane End'. It contains the skeleton of a three bay, oak-framed hall house of c.1450 with the single-storey hall parallel to the road and a bay at each end. A chimney and floors were inserted in the open hall, possibly at the start of the 17th-century. It was re-fronted in the mid-to-late 17th-century for the Steward of the Penn Estate. It is of red brick with blue headers, a first-floor band course and projecting bay. It is a rather official-looking building with an element of formality given by its symmetry on either side of an unusual, small, single bay porch. This was the single central entrance before the house was divided into two in the late 1940s.

Yew Tree House (JT)

Hampdens (JT)

Hampdens (formerly Allandale) is a fine Edwardian house, built in 1907 on what was then an open field, by Walter Evans, the owner of the smithy opposite, (telephone number, Penn 6, in the 1915 directory). In his kitchen garden, which is now the forecourt of Winters Garage, Walter Evans frequently found medieval floor tiles when digging. He also found what he thought was the entrance to an underground passage leading to Penn Church, which, in retrospect, must have been the flue of a kiln.

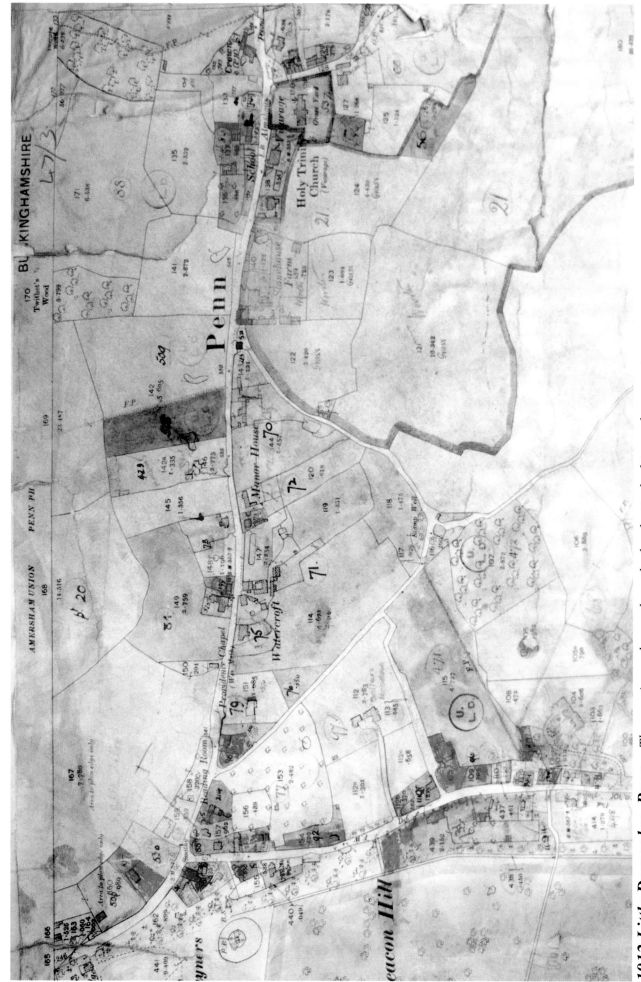

1912 Little Domesday, Penn – *The varying colours show the land attached to each property*

Winters Garage (EM)

Winters (formerly *Shorts* and before that, *Cardens*) *Garage* was built by Walter Garland Carden in 1952. He first started a garage at the Crown in 1931-3 and then moved it to the former coach house of Hampdens, which he later (1955) converted to the 2-bedroom cottage, *White Cottage*, where he still lives today. When petrol tanks were dug by spade, in 1933, half a dozen whole Penn floor tiles and many fragments were found. His Garland grandfather owned the Crown and he inherited both Cobblers and Hampdens. Winters Garage closed in 2006.

Stratfords Cottage (EM)

Wayside (JT)

Regius Court (JT)

To the west of Winters Garage lies a pair of unlisted brick vernacular cottages at right angles to the road. *Stratfords Cottage,* at the front, is timber-framed. It was owned by the Penn Estate until 1957 and in the 1890s was occupied by John Saunders who was bailiff to Mr Wooster the tenant farmer of Puttenham. The cottage went with the farm. It has been considerably extended to the left and this presumably prevented Listing. A possible medieval tile kiln was discovered when digging a cess pit in the front garden in 1939, but was not properly excavated because of the outbreak of war. *Beam Ends* lies behind and presumably shares the same history. It has a date of 1660 inscribed on a tile in a corridor. They both appear on the 1811 OS map and there were no houses between them and the settlement of Tylers Green until new building was encouraged by the opening of the railway at Beaconsfield in1906.

Wayside, The Cranny and Glenmore were all built by Frank Perfect in c.1914. Wayside was Penn Post Office from 1915-20. The first two have tile-hung details. *Regius Court*, formerly a builders' yard for three generations of the Perfect family, and before them the Hancocks, is now an attractively-designed group of office buildings.

Rayners front (EM)

The Rayners Estate

Philip Rose (1816-83) was a remarkable man. He was a solicitor and came from a successful Wycombe family, many of them Mayors. In 1841, when he was still only 25 years old, one of his clerks got TB and he could find no London hospital to take him because 'consumption' was thought to be so contagious. He thereupon organised and inspired his elders to set up the Brompton Hospital, now world famous, with Queen Victoria as the patron. Prince Albert laid the foundation stone, a dozen peers and bishops served on the committee and Charles Dickens spoke on its behalf.

Rayners side (EM)

He then earned a fortune, having persuaded his firm to act for the Great Northern Railway as it expanded its line. He also organised a branch line from Maidenhead to Wycombe with a convenient stop at Loudwater, down to which he constructed a driveway. He was a devoted friend and admirer of Disraeli and managed his legal and financial affairs as well as acting as national agent for the Conservative Party. Both he and Disraeli bought their estates at the same time - Disraeli at Hughenden Manor and Rose at Rayners - and often exchanged visits. Within weeks of becoming Prime Minister in 1874, Disraeli offered him a baronetcy. He was later High Sheriff of the county, as was his son.

Rayners outbuildings (EM)

Rose created his estate from two farms, Rayners and Colehatch in Hammersley Lane, both of which he purchased in 1845, and eventually owned over 550 acres. He ended up as the de facto squire of Tylers Green with Rayners the focus of all village celebrations and nearly two-thirds of the adult population either his estate workers or his tenants. Two hundred would sit down to an annual dinner. In 1854, with his enormous energy and drive and largely his own money, he succeeded in building St Margaret's Church and setting up a separate parish. He also built St Margaret's Institute (see below) and was much

Tiling decoration at Rayners (EM)

Rayners gate and lodge, including the Home Guard's hole in the wall (EM)

Rayners lodge (JT)

Obelisk at Rayners (EM)

involved with the Tylers Green School. He was succeeded by his son, the second Sir Philip, who continued the Rayners' traditions, hosting his last celebration, a grand firework display 'In Celebration of Victory and Peace' at Rayners in July 1919. He died only three months later. His eldest son had recently died of war wounds and the title and estate were inherited by his young grandson whose trustees thought it best to sell off the estate. This was done in 1920, when the house and grounds were bought by the London County Council for use as a school for deaf children.

Rayners (now *Penn School*), is concealed behind a six foot high brick and flint wall with flint caps on the piers. The circular hole in the wall near the main gate was put in by the Home Guard in the Second World War to take one end of a telegraph pole to be used as a roadblock against invading Germans. There were several others around the village, but nothing remains of them. The original gabled Elizabethan-style house was built in 1847 by an unrecorded architect, from bricks made on the spot using clay dug from what is now a large pond in front of the house. It was further extended over the next 20 years, including work in 1868 by David Brandon, the architect of St Margaret's Church. Encaustic tiles decorate the side conservatory, garden gateways and elsewhere. The house was its owner's pride and joy and the elaborate architecture and fine detail of the brickwork is most impressive. It undoubtedly would have been Listed had it not been for the ugly 1960s extension to the rear and should at least be on the Local List.

Rayners Lodge (c.1847) is a decorative mix of red brick with yellow stock dressings and quoining, its steeply pitched tiled roof decorated with fish-scale tiles. The brick gatepost (which lost its wrought iron gates to the war effort in the Second World War) has decorative tile insets, presumably referring back to the area's heritage, although clearly in ignorance of the size and design of an authentic medieval Penn tile. The *obelisk* of Portland stone and polished Peterhead granite records Queen Victoria's visit to Rayners in 1881. She wished to pay homage to Disraeli, her former Prime Minister, by following his last journey from Windsor Castle to Hughenden Manor via Rayners. The obelisk can be glimpsed from the main gate. *The Bothy* (c.1847), further in, is a fine example of a small estate building.

Rayners bothy (EM)

Area 3: Tyler End

The flint wall continues up to the newly-built (1991) brick and flint *Partridge House.* Beyond lies *The Red House**, a substantial dwelling built for modest gentry and occupied in 1841, when it was a smaller house than now, by Thomas Fowler, a man of independent means. It was bought by Philip Rose and was St Margaret's first Parsonage House from 1854 to 1865. The building has since been extended in a grand style, with a semi-octagonal bay at the southern end and ancillary accommodation set to the rear. The main elevation is of vibrant red brick and employs a pale render to great effect. The roof is of slate, hipped, with ridging tiles and decorative brickwork on the chimney stacks. The building has a carved stone stringcourse, sash windows and a grand pedimented porch; detailing to the rear block includes exuberantly carved bargeboards. Glimpses of the house are obtained through the tall hedge that lines the roadside.

The Red House (EM)

View across King's green (JT)

Tyler End, Penn shopping area

Opposite the Red House, across a small green , and on the other side of a high beech hedge, which it used to be said 'divided the village' because it roughly marks the parish boundary, is a cluster of former shops and houses. These are set along the first part of Elm Road, which here is just a small lane to the Red Lion deliberately bypassed by the main road, once known as the 'horse road'. The tilers' kilns extended up the east side of Elm Road towards Potters Cross. A close cluster of shops and a pub (the Red Lion) developed at the southern end. This area now has nine 17th and 18th-century Listed Buildings of varied design and appearance and remains quiet and unspoilt. Woodbridges, a grocer/baker and King's, a butcher, survived into the 1980s. Many of the original shopfronts are still retained and a bookshop and newly-arrived music shop (formerly a general store) are welcome survivors.

The range of architectural styles here is varied, from the timber-framed Stratfords, Gable Cottage and April Cottage, to the grander Dilehurst and Kings with 18th-century detailing and retained shopfront. Cotters Barn, set well back, is older in style, a good example of a 17th-century lobby entrance house. The unlisted buildings are in a vernacular, late 19th-century style, of brick, flint or white-painted.

There is some uncertainty about dating since there are no buildings at all shown on maps of 1761 and 1770 from Beacon Hill to opposite Widmer Pond. Buildings in this area first appear on the 1800 and 1811 maps. However, we must assume that the maps are wrong since several of the Listed Buildings are dated architecturally to the 17th-century or earlier; there was an alehouse-keeper listed at a Red Lion, presumably this one, when licensing records first started in 1753; and the former butcher's shop claims to have been established in 1782.

2 Regius Court (EM)

At the southern end of this shopping area, there is a picturesque terrace of three very varied buildings set back from the road and facing a small green. The first is a small brick & flint cottage, *2 Regius Court*, which used to be *Perfect's office*** and is still in use as an office; it was let to Lloyds Bank for one day a week in the 1930s. In the centre, *Stratfords*** has two stories and four bays, and is apparently an 18th-century rebuilding of a medieval house since part of a cruck truss remains inside. The house has unusual tripartite casements and a plain but attractive door hood and dominates the group by virtue of height and mass. *Gable Cottage*** is brick, 18th-century and has two gabled, eaves-breaking windows to the front with wooden bargeboards. Evidence of timber-framing can be seen on the northern gable end.

Stratfords and Gable Cottage (EM)

Kings**, a butcher's shop until 1982, retains not only its attractive shop window under a hood, but also the iron hooks for hanging meat. The double gables of the single storey shop unit face on to the road, and have carved brickwork to the eaves. The main house is set back from the road and has a stringcourse and good sash windows. There is a notice on the shop front 'Established 1782' and 'TCW 1797' is painted on a brick at the front, which probably stands for Thomas and Charlotte Weller. He was a Penn butcher in 1780 and her father held Puttenham Farm. The King family, father and son, ran the shop for over 75 years, from before 1864 to after 1939. Penn Post Office was here, in 1871, but only for a year or two. The weather-boarded barn to the south of Kings is a 1985 replacement for a former slaughterhouse which burnt down. It remains a functional structure, built right up to the road edge.

Kings (EM)

A courtyard between Kings and *Dilehurst*** makes a break in the building line here which again adds variety to the street scene. The protruding main 18th-century house is of dark header brickwork, with red stretcher bond dressings, indicative of a high-status building, although the brickwork is a refacing of an older internal structure with some evidence of timber-framing. Its public face has four sash windows and evidence of a blocked door and window; the entrance to the building is actually on the side under a pedimented hood. Also on the side elevation new windows have been inserted.

View down Elm Road (JT)

Dilehurst (EM)

30

Strings **, the newly-opened music shop, is attached to Dilehurst and shares its roof span – indeed the original shop was inserted into the building and there is evidence of timber framing within. It has a good Victorian front veranda from its use as Day's, a grocer/draper from the 1880s, succeeded by Baddeley & Son as a general store from c.1920 until the 1960s. There was a notice on the front advertising 'Close and open carriages let on hire' and 'Brougham for hire'. It was an antiques shop until 1993.

Strings (EM)

The 17th and 18th-century *Cotters Barn* **, roughcast and brick, is set back from the road and is a lobby entrance house built around a central chimney stack. It has white-painted segmental window arches on the ground floor. The stables housed the horses for the village carrier service. Cathleen Nesbitt, the actress, lived there with her husband Cecil Ramage. *The Cottage Bookshop* *, which stands to the front of Cotters Barn, is 19th-century and is of brick with slate roofs. It was built as a private house, but has been successively, a fish shop, briefly Barclays Bank, an electrical shop and a shoe repairer and has been a bookshop since 1951. *One Chimney* ** is 18th-century and is a very quaint brick and tile building with a single casement to the front and eaves-breaking dormer.

Cotters Barn (EM)

April Cottage ** is 17th-century and basically timber-framed, but refaced at the front in red and purple chequer brick with a stringcourse. The brick and flint wall on the south side beyond the chimney stack creates a void and conceals a substantial timber-framed wall with wattle and daub infill which looks as though it was once connected to an adjoining cottage using the same shared chimney stack. The sharp jump in the ridge of the roof supports this suggestion. The rear gable is all timber-framed with brick infill panels.

The Cottage Bookshop (JT)

April Cottage (EM)

April Cottage showing timber-framing at the back (EM)

One Chimney (JT)

Penn Barn (JT)

Former Woodbridges buildings (JT)

Woodbridges Cottage (EM)

Across the road, there is a terrace of buildings which were once all part of Woodbridges, described in 1920 as 'grocer, baker, corndealer and jobmaster Phone 19 Penn'. Deeds go back to 1800 and there is mention of a shop in 1824. The Wheeler family owned the business, which included Penn Post Office, for 70 odd years from before 1847 until it was bought by the Woodbridges in 1915. The Wheelers took Penn Post Office with them when they moved to a new house, Wayside, in Church Road, in 1915.

Penn Barn, is a late-Victorian barn lying at right angles to the road and was for 30 years a gallery selling paintings, old prints and books, but is now an office. Earlier, it housed the traps for the horse bus service to Beaconsfield. Its roof was raised 20 years ago. *The Granary* was used as a storeroom and in the 1930s as a shop.

Old Stores Cottage was the Woodbridges' bakehouse and the bread oven had a date 1846 stamped on it. Bread was baked in it until 1964. *Emily's Cottage* was part of the bakers' house. *Woodbridges Cottage* incorporates the former grocery shop which closed amidst champagne and lamentations in 1986. The central part of this terrace steps back from the road slightly, creating a sense of an enclosure.

Red Lion Cottages, a pair of early-Victorian brick cottages, are adjacent to the *Red Lion** and look out on to Widmer Pond and the Front Common. The deeds of the Red Lion go back to 1770 and the pub is named on the first list of alehouse keepers in 1753. The building is 18th-century and later, with two storeys, a tile roof and dentil brick eaves. The building has a flat-roofed 1930s extension to the front, fortunately softened by judicious planting. What may just possibly have been the former carriage arch is still visible over the window on the right hand side of the front elevation, and there is a tiled offset to the massive chimney stack. The building is part-fronted by a brick and flint wall. The Court of Segraves Manor used to meet there in the 18th and 19th-centuries.

Red Lion (EM)

Red Lion Cottages (JT)

Widmer Pond (JT)

Widmer Pond is arguably the focal point for the joint Conservation Area. It is one of a series of ponds marking the parish, district and deanery boundaries (Pistles Pond and Wash Pond, both in Beacon Hill, are others). They have done so unchanged since the ponds marked the divide between the Saxon Hundreds of Burnham and Desborough well over 1,000 years ago. Widmer probably means 'wide pond' in Old English and nearby fields took the same name.

The pond was used for washing clothes, but not for drinking-water, which came either from roof water collected in underground tanks in every cottage garden, from a spring at Stumpwell off Beacon Hill, or in times of drought, from a 350-foot-deep well at Rayners. The concern used to be to keep the water clean, and vociferous complaint was made if ducks were allowed on the pond. The Victorian pump was installed in 1989 in memory of Ken Stevens, a long-time chairman of CWPC.

Old Bank House (EM)

*The Old Bank House*** lies the other side of Putts Lane leading to Puttenham Place. This substantial, two-and-a-half-storey late 17th-century building is rather grand in comparison with the vernacular buildings that lie adjacent and is a focal point in views across the Front Common. Its most striking feature is the twin curvilinear Dutch gables to the front and to either side. It is supposed that it was once, together with Pewsey Cottage, one of the two lodges to Puttenham Place which was built as a small manor house and was itself encased in brick, c.1680, and is thought then to have had similar Dutch gables. The Puttenhams had sold their house to the Butterfields a century earlier, and Mathew Butterfield, around 1680, was easily the second largest landowner in the parish after the Penn family. In the early 1900s, the Old Bank House was divided into two cottages and was Barclays Bank for about three years in the early 1930s. An architect owner then rebuilt the right front and side. It was previously called The Little House. Built of chequer brick, red with grey headers, it has brick band courses at first and second floor level and fine moulded brickwork to the gables themselves. The windows are leaded-light wooden casement style. It needs hardly be said that it was never a hunting lodge of Henry VIII and neither did Catherine of Aragon live at Puttenham while awaiting her divorce from Henry VIII.

Puttenham Place, front (EM)

Puttenham Place, back (EM)

The Elms, with Gladstone's caricature (EM)

Caricature of Gladstone (EM)

Development along Elm Road, between the Old Bank House and the Sports Club, is characterised by groups of Listed cottages, with four later brick detached houses on infill sites between. These are: *Merchants Yard* (formerly Elmside), built by Frank Perfect (1924), and with George Slade's coal-merchant's yard at the rear from the 1930s until the 1960s; *St Mark's Cottage* (1931); *Pond House* (1939); and *The Elms* (1931). All face the Front Common with a wide verge of common land separating the building plots from the road. The Elms has a caricature on the ridge of the front gable of William Gladstone (1809-98), the Liberal Prime Minister. It is a very good likeness, but in a fool's cap with a rat's body. He was Prime Minister for some 14 years between 1868 and 1894 and this caricature came from Rayners where it advertised Sir Philip Rose's hostility to Gladstone who was the great political rival of Rose's friend Benjamin Disraeli (1804-81), the Tory leader and Prime Minister.

Tylers Green House (the mansion). The most interesting house in Penn is no longer there. A large medieval, timber-framed mansion house, with over 20 rooms and 15 hearths, stood opposite the lower end of Widmer Pond. A deed of 1493 refers to a house in Tylerend and a document of 1512 makes it clear that it was a hall house with a tiled

Tylers Green House, the mansion
(Bodleian Library)

Daniel Baker II, the diarist (1661-1727) (Christies, from portrait owned by Richard Hewer)

roof. It was one of only two 'seats' listed in the parish in 1720 (Penn Place, now called Penn House, was the other) and was known variously as Penn House and Tylers Green House. It was occupied by many interesting people. Thomas Long, the County Coroner in the mid-1600s, who was married to the daughter of the last Puttenham to live at Puttenham Place; Gulielma Springett, who was the wife-to-be of William Penn the Quaker and founder of Pennsylvania, wrote to him in 1670 that 'deare George Fox (the founder of Quakerism) was heare att two of our meetings and they were very large'; Sir Nathaniel Curzon and his wife Sarah Penn, heiress to the Penn Estate and six times great grandparents of the present Earl Howe; Daniel Baker, High Sheriff of the County in 1721, who kept a diary of his time in the house, and whose family owned it for 80 years until a grand sale in 1769 when the contents of every room were revealed in the sale brochure. The diary and many Baker family letters can be seen in the Records Office at Aylesbury. There are two fine monuments to the family in Penn Church.

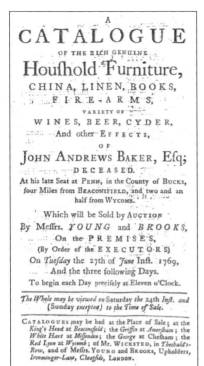

Sale of the mansion in 1769

In 1726, Daniel Baker obtained an agreement from the lord of Bassetsbury Manor to 'rail and beautify' the common by 'planting elm or other trees in Walks, Rows, Knolls or Clumps' on the 'Wast Ground of Tylering Green' – in effect to create a park in front of the mansion house. Similar agreements in 1740 and 1745 with the manors of first Penn then Bassetsbury, allowed his son to plant trees extending 'as far as the Gravel Pit lying west from the said Mansion about two hundred yards' (i.e. to the clay pit around which Bank Road now circles); then down as far as Potters Cross (sometimes referred to as Potters Lane Bottom); and up beyond 'Great Widmore Pond', which he was allowed to stock with 'Carp, Tench or other Fish'.

Martha Baker (1668-1752), wife of the diarist (Christies, from portrait owned by Richard Hewer)

The elms of Elm Road c.1910 'God First' can just be seen

The 1761 Rocque map shows four rows of trees in front of the house, but they stop far short of Potters Cross, probably because the first enclosure on the Front Common had already been made by the future owner of the Old Bell House in 1746. When the elm trees lining Elm Road were finally cut down in 1977, they were estimated to be about 125 years old and so were presumably planted after the 1852 Penn Inclosure Award which gave the common to local inhabitants. There was then no mansion house owner to look after the trees on the common and any surviving old elms would have been cut down and new ones planted, but only along the roadside. It was this second generation of elms which gave the name to Elm Road. It was only the presence of the mansion that had prevented encroachment and building on the common opposite and so bequeathed us our open common as well as the elm trees.

General Haviland (1717-84), a veteran of many wars, lived in Tylers Green House after the Baker family. He was involved in defeating Bonnie Prince Charlie in 1745 and commanded a brigade in Canada, serving under Wolfe at the capture of Quebec from the French in 1759. There is a fine monument to him in Penn Church with an epitaph by his friend Edmund Burke - 'An experienced and successful Commander without ostentation: a firm friend without profession: a good man without pretence.'

General Haviland
(Regimental Museum, Royal Irish Regiment)

Finally, the old mansion became the French School - the school for boys of the émigré French nobility, founded in 1796 by Edmund Burke, a leading parliamentarian of his day. The Comte d'Artois, the future Charles X of France, was its patron and came to the school to present prizes. Other visitors included a past and future Prime Minister of England, the Lord Chancellor and the Minister at War, as well as a stone-throwing anti-French mob who tore down a wall and broke the windows. The school closed in 1820 and the house was pulled down two years later. The 1838 Tithe Map shows that the fields adjoining the road from the Red Lion down to the former doctors' surgery, and back to include the football ground were all called French House Mead.

Edmund Burke (1729-97)

Holiness Mission (former infants' school) (David Wooster)

Well End, Mid Elm and 3 Elm Cottage (EM)

Kenilworth and Japonica (EM)

The Chestnuts and Snowdrop Cottage (EM)

Only the former stable of Tylers Green House survived. This became an infants' school in 1840 and for two-and-a-half years was also home to Tylers Green School before the new building on School Road was opened in 1876. The stable was still an infants' school in the 1890s, but its last use, from January 1906, was as a nonconformist chapel led by Mr George Wooster (tenant of Penbury Farm from 1889), and known as the *Holiness Mission*. 'God First' was painted on the side at this time. The future President Hoover of the United States shared the same evangelical enthusiasm and visited Penbury Farm before the First World War. George Wooster left Penn in 1938 and the building was pulled down in c.1939 when Pond House was built.

The three groups of attractive Penn Estate cottages provided by the first Earl Howe in 1848–50 stand on the land occupied by the mansion house and its extensive gardens. They are of coursed flint with brick dressings and architectural detailing including hood moulds to windows, porches, quoins, and slate roofs with central chimneys. A terrace of three, *Well End***, *Mid Elm*** and *3 Elm Cottage***, has a central projecting bay with stacks to either side and date stone marked 1850. *Kenilworth*** and *Japonica*** are simpler in appearance but have decorative porches. They have no date stone, but appear on an 1852 map. *The Chestnuts*** and *Snowdrop Cottage*** (formerly *Collaine*) pick up the local Dutch gable motif in brick and flint and have a date stone marked 1848.

French Meadow** lies further along Elm Road. It is 17th-century, timber-framed, clad in 18th-century brick with a tile roof. A large modern (c.1961) extension was added to the left of the gable. The original house was already a fairly substantial building of two bays with a crosswing and may have been a farmhouse associated with the neighbouring mansion house (Green Farm appears in old records). Many Elizabeth I coins were found by a metal detector in the garden. It seems that a tiny, one-bedroom cottage was added to the right of the chimney stack, probably in the 19th-century. Mr Griffen, builder of the St Margaret's Parish Room, lived in the main house, and there was a blacksmith with his forge, a wheelwright and a carpenter in the yard in the front. It is now one house again and is set back within the plot and so creates an important gap in the street scene. You can see Harrow-on-the-Hill from upstairs at the back of the house.

French Meadow (EM)

A *horse chestnut tree*, very old and hollow, stands on the common verge outside French Meadow. Harold Wheeler, now 101, remembers playing in the tree as a small child when it looked much the same as it does now. He could go inside and right through it even then. When all the old elm trees, which gave Elm Road its name, were struck by disease and cut down in 1977, Harold made a special plea for the horse chestnut in case it was removed with its neighbours.

The open common ends at this point and buildings once again cluster along both sides of the road. At the entrance to the Sports Club, new houses, *Rose Cottages*, have replaced a late Victorian pair which burned down in 2000. They have been built on the site of a consecutive series of five kilns, which were probably in use from the 15th to 17th-centuries although 14th-century floor tiles were also found on the site.

The hollow horse chestnut tree (EM)

1 and 2 Yew Tree Cottages*, have fine flint work with brick dressings and were estate cottages. Then there is *Mayfields*, a neat 1951 bungalow; a terrace of four fine Arts and Crafts-style cottages (1910), *Summer Cottage, Lyndhurst, Roseneath* and *Greenhurst*; and *Yonder Lodge Cottage,* a mid-Victorian brick cottage, which went with Yonder Lodge.

Yonder Lodge** lies at the northern end of the Conservation Area. It is early 19th-century, built as a small country house of painted brick, with associated stabling and outbuildings some distance to the south. It has three storeys, the side wings have Venetian windows and the central windows are blind. The building is set back within its grounds and partly screened by boundary trees. Its front gates were lost to the war effort in 1940. Sir Oliver Millar, former Surveyor of the Queen's Pictures, lived there for nearly 40 years from 1958 before moving to the Back Common. Yonder was a racehorse belonging to a previous owner. The house was earlier known as Penwood Lodge and earlier still as Park Place.

1 & 2 Yew Tree Cottages (JT)

Summer Cottage, Lyndhurst, Roseneath and Greenhurst (EM)

Yonder Lodge Cottage (EM)

Yonder Lodge (JT)

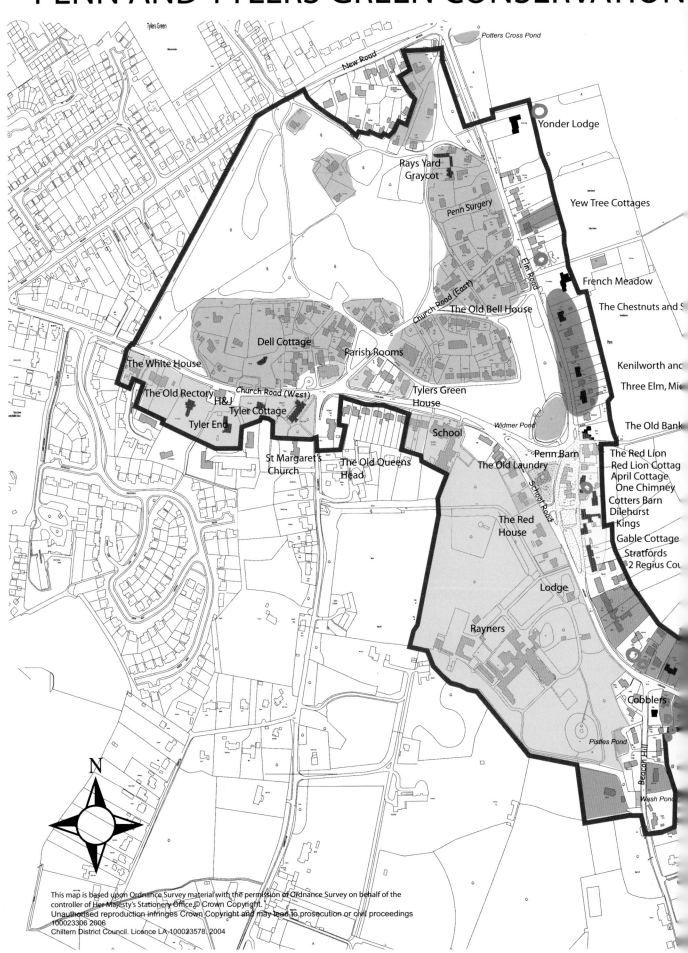

Tylers Green

Potters Cross Pond

New Road

Yonder Lodge

Rays Yard
Graycot

Yew Tree Cottages

Penn Surgery

French Meadow

Church Road (East)

The Old Bell House

The Chestnuts and S

Dell Cottage

The White House

Parish Rooms

Kenilworth and

Three Elm, Mi

The Old Rectory

Church Road (West)

Tylers Green
House

The Old Bank

H&J

Tyler Cottage

Widmer Pond

Penn Barn

The Red Lion

Tyler End

School

Red Lion Cottag
April Cottage
One Chimney

St Margaret's
Church

The Old Queens
Head

The Old Laundry

Cotters Barn
Dilehurst
Kings

The Red
House

Gable Cottage

Stratfords
2 Regius Cou

Lodge

Rayners

Cobblers

School Road

Elm Road

Pistles Pond

Beacon Hill

Wash Pond

N

KEY

- Penn village around the church
- 17th-19th century higher status
- Medieval tile industry sites
- 18th and 19th century commercial/shops
- Mainly 19th century encroachments
- Buildings associated with Penn Estate
- Buildings associated with Rayners
- Post 1906 railway infill
- Former extent of Commons

WYCOMBE DISTRICT COUNCIL

Chiltern District Council

Puttenham Place Farm

Putts Lane

Free Methodist Chapel

Penn Cottage

The Chinnery

Watercroft

Watercroft Pond

Manor House

Troutwells and Pewsey Cottage

Grove's Barn

Long Pond

Stonehouse

Church Road (Penn)

Church Hall

South View

The Old Vicarage

Holy Trinity Church

The Knoll

The Crown

Crown Cottage

Hatchits

Pauls Hill Cottages

Pauls Hill

Stumpwell

Scale

1/4 mile

Victoria Cottages (EM)

Jackson Howes, estate agents (EM)

Victoria House (JT)

On the west side of Elm Road all the houses are 19th-century, standing on earlier encroachments on the common and none are Listed. A brick terrace, *1-7 Victoria Cottages*, was built in c.1975. Their predecessors, popularly known as Cabbage Row, were cottages built with materials from the old French School. They lie between the modern *Burntwood*, and the red and yellow brick of the late Victorian building, a butcher's shop (until 1988), but now estate agent *Jackson Howes*. North of the Church Road junction there is a run of 19th-century cottages. *Victoria House* is cream-painted brick with a pretty door hood. It was a Wellers of Amersham beerhouse called The Victoria (1868-1919), replacing The Travellers Friend, first licensed in 1830, which lay further back from Elm Road behind the Bethlehem Meeting Hall in what is now the garden of Blue Gates. The original copper bar and serving hatch is still in place. The Victoria was also briefly a grocer's shop in the early 1900s. The new Vicar of Penn lodged there in the early 1920s while waiting for his new vicarage to be built in Paul's Hill.

The new Penn Surgery (EM)

Baytree Cottage, of brick and flint, and *Hillcrest Cottage* are a mid-Victorian terrace. These buildings are unified by the use of slate on the roofs, and this feature has been picked up on the architecture of the new (2005) *Penn Surgery*, which replaced the *Horse & Groom*, a public house from 1832. There used to be a pre-1840 cottage in the new surgery's car park towards the back of the site. *The Old Bakehouse* has deeds back to 1826 when it had half an acre with a bakehouse, stable, and coachhouse. The 1811 map shows a building in that area; there was a baker living there in 1841, and bread was baked in a sack oven until 1928. The house is brick and flint with painted render on the front elevations and a slate roof.

The former Horse & Groom
(Bernard Saunders)

The Old Bakehouse (EM)

Baytree Cottage and Hillcrest Cottage (EM)

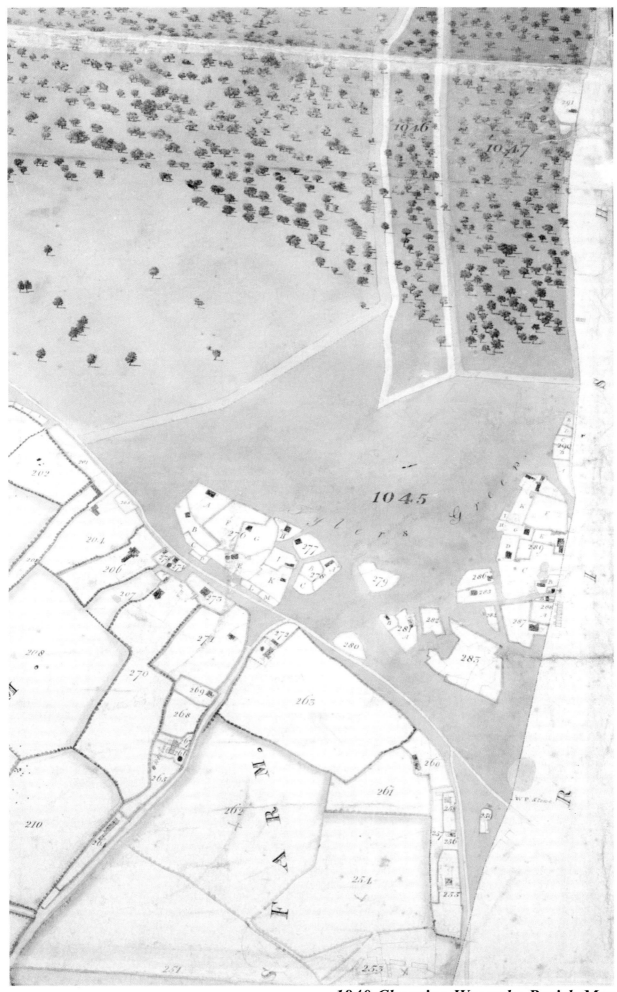

1840 Chepping Wycombe Parish Map

41

Tylers Green Common -

encroachment and settlement by snatch-holders - the illegal settlement of Tylers Green Common

Until the middle of the 19th-century, Tyler End Green was part of a 4,000-acre common of heath and woodland which stretched over seven parishes, its perimeter or 'ends' marked by small settlements such as Widmer End, Heath End, Spurlings End, Mop End, Beamond End and, of course, Tyler End. Before the time of the 14th-century tilers, Tyler End was called Garrett Green (corrupted to 'Gerrards Green' in later manor rolls), which seems to be from an old French word meaning 'watchtower' and may have referred to the beacon. If so, it was a post-Conquest name. Earlier still, in Saxon times, Tyler End may have been called Hammersley, meaning 'hill clearing' (Old English *hamor*, a hill; *lēah*, open space in a wood). The pond and the common are split by the parish border with the major part of the common on the Wycombe side, which for many centuries was owned by Bassetsbury Manor, named after its first early 13th-century lord, Alan Basset. Penn Manor held the other side.

The Penn Manor Court Rolls show that during the 18th-century the sharp rise in population had resulted in a large number of small encroachments throughout the parish, nibbling away at road verges and between houses. Generally the encroachers were ordered to throw the land open to the commons again, on pain of a double fine. This was not always enforced and the encroachment was tolerated if the encroacher paid an annual fine, which was repeated year after year and signed an acknowledgement that they owed a quit rent for the land. In many cases the rent was so small it was not worth collecting and, if no action was taken, in due course a possessory title could be claimed by the 'snatch-holder'. Counsels in court cases in 1796 and 1829 maintained that 12 years' quiet possession of land without any check or acknowledgement by the lord of the manor gave a good title to the land, although a case law precedent of 20 years was also quoted.

We can trace the progress of early encroachment on a series of maps:
1761 - The earliest map with sufficient detail shows the only enclosures of land were along the side of Elm Road from the Old Bell House down to the present Rays Lane. There were no buildings anywhere on the Front or Back Common and open common continued half way down Beacon Hill as far as the site of the former beacon.

1777 - The Old Bell House was the only building on the common.
1800 - An accurate military map shows the Old Bell House and behind it, a predecessor of Jackson Howes, the estate agent. There was also a small enclosure with buildings on it opposite the end of Hammersley Lane, reached by what is now Nursery Lane.
1811 - There were now buildings on the common along Elm Road, and also in a larger enclosure opposite St Margaret's Church in which Lost Cottage, Dell Cottage and Truro Cottage now stand. The Woodbridge shop area had been enclosed and built upon, and there were buildings on the Laundry Cottage enclosure.
1824 – Little change

This pattern of development is confirmed by surviving deeds and is the consequence of the sudden growth of the Wycombe chair industry, in the late 1790s. The 50-acre common was then owned by absentee landlords, the Dean and Canons of Windsor, who were Lords of the Manor of Bassetsbury. Standing at Widmer Pond, there would have been an uninterrupted view across a common full of clay pits to the southern edge of St John's Wood. The edge of the wood is still marked by an open ride along the edge of the common from Ashley Drive towards Wheeler Avenue. During the following seventy or so years, illegal enclosure of about 25 acres took place, mainly by artisans and agricultural labourers. They started by building 'mud houses' in or close to the clay pits, gradually replacing them by small brick and flint cottages, mostly 2 up and 2 down with an outside privy, and often in pairs or terraced. They had no mains water or bathroom and were built for as little as £40. The present, apparently random, layout of small tracks and plots on both Front and Back Commons was largely dictated by the clay pits. It is only on the edges of the common that more substantial houses are found.

'Within living memory Tyler's Green was an open common without any house or building on it', wrote Philip Rose to the Deans and Canons of Windsor in May 1854, *'but small encroachments were from time to time made upon the Waste at the skirt of the great Wood (St John's Wood) on which mud houses were afterwards built which have gradually given place to buildings of a more substantial character, until within 40 or 50 years a population has grown upon the Waste of several hundred souls with houses built closely together wherever a spot of ground could be safely enclosed...a population now of nearly 600 is comprised within the space of quarter a mile.*

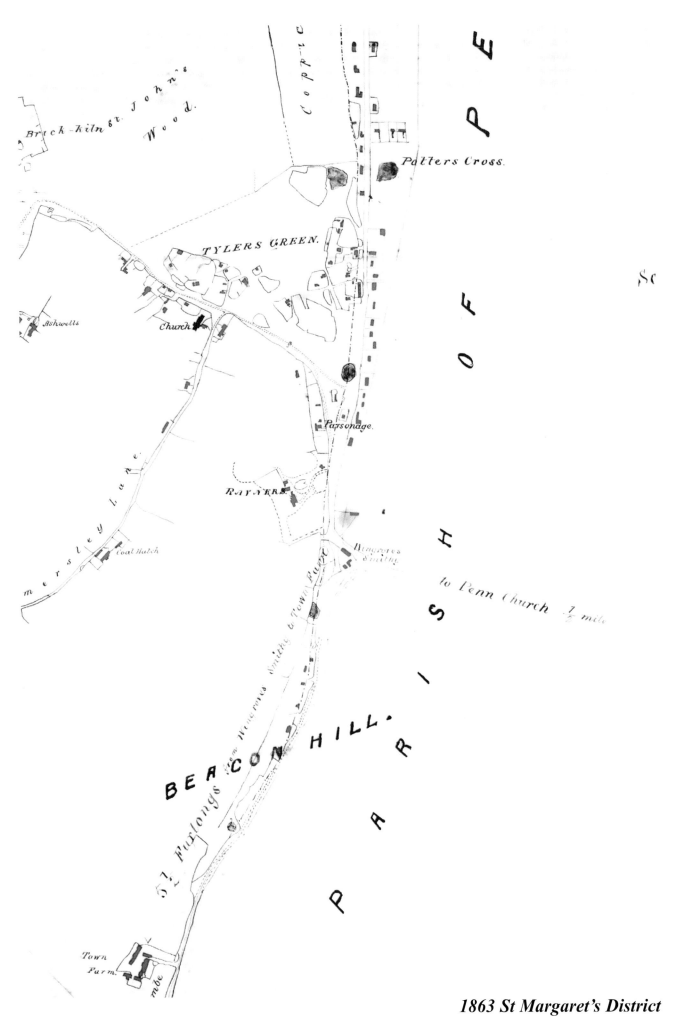

1863 St Margaret's District

The new district also took in part of Penn Parish. The Tylers Green side is based on the 1848 Wycombe Tithe Map

It will be difficult to point to any other instance where a population has been collected so rapidly by illegal means and with so little resistance on the part of the owners of the soil...loud complaints from the neighbourhood & some warning notices... but empty threats...so in the estimation of the inhabitants the encroachments have acquired a security little short of the most legal tenure.

There has been rapid growth before but at an increasing pace in the last few years...in the last two years nearly 20 new cottages have been erected on the common...at the present moment there are preparations for encroachments not of feet or yards but of roods and poles...in one instance approximately an acre.

The only means of stopping it is by an Enclosure of the Common which is now being promoted in earnest by adjoining proprietors & it is understood that the Deans & Canons cordially support. It is clear that under no Enclosure can existing buildings be removed. The population is necessarily of a low & degraded class, for the most part extremely ignorant and needing most careful and judicious treatment.'

The immediate urgency for an enclosure of the common was that Earl Howe, whose agreement was essential to the success of Rose's project to build St Margaret's Church, had said that enclosure of the Wycombe Wastes should be 'contemporaneous' with the building. Rose also pointed out to the Dean and Canons that enclosure would considerably increase the value of their property. This was because former common land was allotted in parcels to the private ownership of the lord of the manor and surrounding landowners on a *pro rata* basis i.e., the bigger the landowner, the bigger the allotment. However, 'numerous obstacles arose', amongst them the fact that for well over a century the Dean and Canons had leased the common to the Dashwood family of West Wycombe and so Sir George Dashwood had the prime responsibility for preventing encroachments.

It is interesting to compare Philip Rose's account with the Tylers Green censuses for 1841 and 1851. In 1841 there were 345 people in 81 households. In 1851, there were 402 people in 97 households, with an average age of 25, a mean family size of 4 and a very high birthrate in the previous five years. About half were born in Wycombe parish (which then included Tylers Green) and over three quarters were born within a five mile radius. There was an unusually high number (42%) of craftsmen (chair turners, sawyers or carpenters) and a similar number of agricultural labourers. A quarter of the women were lacemakers. Only five households were of independent means. Interestingly, 53 heads of households, well over half, had arrived in the previous 10 years, two thirds of them in their 20s and 30s, even though only 16 additional households had been formed, i.e. at a rate of $1\frac{1}{2}$ each year. Sixteen of them were chair turners, sawyers or carpenters, of whom there had been only three in 1841, and 18 were agricultural labourers.

The picture in 1851 is therefore of a young, mostly local, very mobile community with a high proportion of skills for the chair industry. Three years later, Philip Rose was clearly exaggerating both their numbers, by including the Penn side, and their 'degraded class', in order to strengthen his argument for enclosure and the need for a new church. He did the same with the results of a census on religious attendance, which he conducted in 1849, in order to demonstrate the need for a new Anglican church. He concluded that over half had replied 'nowhere' (i.e. they didn't go to church anywhere) and that only one fifth was Anglican, the remainder being Methodist or Baptist. A more careful analysis would have shown that about a quarter were 'nowheres' and a quarter Anglican. Nonetheless, his message that a once-empty common was rapidly filling with illegal encroachments was accurate.

As Philip Rose noted in 1854, neighbouring proprietors were going ahead with enclosures of common land. Penn parish was surveyed in 1852 with final enclosure in 1855. The Penn part of the Common along Elm Road down to Potters Cross was already illegally enclosed and built on; but the many small private 'allotments' newly created by the enclosure all along the newly defined Hazlemere Road were now potential building plots. Rose also noted the surge of illegal enclosures and building on the Wycombe side of the Common in the early 1850s. This was no doubt stimulated by the 1848 Wycombe Tithe Award, finally agreed in 1849, which mapped the enclosures and would have encouraged more confidence in legal ownership by describing most of them as gardens. There may also have been a fear that the Dean and Canons would soon follow Penn with an Inclosure Award on the Wycombe side. Because of legal uncertainty, plots sometimes changed hands for only a few pounds, as we shall see later. Builders, butchers and publicans, and later, fruiterers, seem to have done particularly well during these years of expansion.

In the event, Tylers Green Common was never enclosed and so the opportunity for illegal enclosure

1875 25 inch O.S. Map

45

continued into the 1870s. In 1876, when the new school was opened, Philip Rose noted that the population of the new parish of St Margaret's had reached 471 in 118 houses on the Tylers Green side and 319 in 69 houses on the Penn side. About half the 50-acre common had been lost to encroachment. We shall see later that the deeds for the earliest cottages relied on statutory declarations by an elderly villager. It was the passing of an Act in 1826 which allowed declarations in place of the earlier requirement for oaths and affirmations in front of a magistrate and the later Statutory Declarations Act of 1835, which is still in use today, which first allowed a title for land to be acquired in this way. An elderly local, writing in about 1960, remembered the popular belief that until about 90 years earlier, if a man could fence or grow a hedge around a plot of common land and keep it for 20 years, it was his own.

In 1868, the 370-acre St John's Wood, which was still part of Wycombe Heath and owned by the Crown, was finally enclosed and there seem to have been only very small encroachments thereafter. The Inclosure Award included the creation of two new 'Public Carriage Roads', St John's (Wood) Road and New Road, lined by small private allotments on which, forty years later, houses started to be built. Most of Tylers Green and a good part of Hazlemere have since been built on the former St John's Wood. The detailed definition of boundaries on and around the Back Common is still much the same today as shown on the first large-scale OS map of 1875.

In 1854, labourers working on St Margaret's Church were being paid 3/6d daily, i.e. about £1 per week. The great majority rented their cottages, but to buy one in 1854 would have cost about £40, nine months' wages. Compare their situation with today's purchaser. Two years ago, one of the five former Woodbine Cottages was up for sale at £335,000. The modern income equivalent of the labourer is probably the lower end of the clerical scale at about £15,000 pa. It would take the modern clerk 22 years' wages to buy the cottage, 30 times more than in 1854.

These sky-high modern prices for brick and flint cottages would have mystified our Victorian predecessors. 'Wretched' and 'inferior' were the descriptions of such small cottages in 1882 and they were given derogatory names like Toe Rag Row, Cabbage Row and Woodbine (there were five cigarettes in a workman's 2d packet). A superior cottage would be built of brick or, at the very least, with a brick front and brick and flint sides and rear.

Wren Cottage in Beacon Hill is a good example of this. Truro Cottage in Nursery Lane seems to be an example of an intermediate stage where a brick skin surrounds a brick and flint interior wall.

The Penn side of the common was enclosed in 1855 and set aside for 'the exercise and recreation of the inhabitants', but as has already been noted, Tylers Green Common was never enclosed. In 1908, Chepping Wycombe Parish Council rented it from the Church Commissioners, who were lords of Bassetsbury Manor, and then purchased it for a nominal £100 in 1954. Deeds for older properties can include the right to pasture – for instance, Dell Cottage, opposite St Margaret's Church. Goats, geese and occasional horses continued to graze on the common up to the 1960s. Common rights were not formally extinguished until 1976 when registration as Village Green was confirmed.

By 1900, the population of Tylers Green had risen to about 900 and in 1906 there was a sale in small lots of the former St John's Wood in response to demand created by the new railway at Beaconsfield. But development was slow and there were still only 1,000 inhabitants in 1916. A newly-arrived war widow noted that 'excluding the vicarage, there are but four people of substance living here'. In 1919, there was a further sale of St John's Wood and there was steady development along Hazlemere Road, New Road and St John's Road. It was not until 1957 that the extensive building started with the first houses of the Deer Park Estate, in Ashley Drive and King's Ride. The population of Tylers Green today is about 4,500, of whom 85% live on what used to be a part of Wycombe Heath.

1908 Map of Tylers Green Common - *when first leased from the Church Commissioners*
Based on map survey of 1897

Looking towards the Old Bell House (JT)

Area 4: Front Common

Some buildings stand out as important in long-range views across the common; the Red Lion and its neighbours to the east; Tylers Green House to the west; the Old Bell House to the north; and the fine Victorian school to the south. We shall circle the Front Common clockwise starting on School Road.

Philip Rose acquired the terrace of four (now three) 'recently erected' *Laundry Cottages* in 1849. They are faced with red brick, with flint to the side and rear, and slate roofs with a dominant single chimney stack. Map evidence shows that earlier houses were first built there on the open common soon after 1800 and so it was an early encroachment, later validated by being recognised by the 1848 Tithe Award. In c.1849, Rose added *The Old Laundry* next to School Road. It is a single-storey brick and flint structure with Dutch gables, also in brick and flint, at both ends and terracotta detailing on the roof. Two big rooms are remembered, one for washing and one for ironing. The pretty building is surrounded by a low brick and flint wall.

The Old Laundry (JT)

Hamilton House, in School Road, was built in 1970 on the site of a much older pre-1840 cottage. *St Margaret's* in green roughcast and *Silvester Cottage* in cream are divisions of a substantial standard mid-Victorian house, *St Margaret's Cottage*, named in an 1871 directory and owned by Philip Rose by 1876. This house was built, probably by Rose, sometime after 1863 when the map shows a much smaller house on the site, and was presumably named after his wife. His granddaughter was living in the house from before 1911 until 1920. The house has a slate roof, a classically inspired porch and an unusually castellated single-storey extension set against a backdrop of mature trees within Rayners park.

St Margaret's and Silvester Cottage (JT)

Elizabeth von Arnim, the author of a novel 'Elizabeth and her German Garden', very popular in its day, who later became Elizabeth, Countess

Russell, apparently also lived there at some time. She may have been a tenant in the early 1900s after her first husband died. When the house was divided in 1960 by Veronica Papworth (see *Stonehouse* earlier), she named the two houses Elizabeth's Garden and Elizabeth's Cottage because, she explained, she had seen Elizabeth's name on the deeds.. There are two adjacent plaques to Elizabeth Russell and her brother, Sir Sydney Beauchamp (of Salters Meadow, Beacon Hill), on the outside south-west wall of St Margaret's Church.

Threshers and café (JT)

The two neighbouring shops, currently *Threshers* and a small café, are housed in a renovated late Victorian draper's shop that was Penn's first telephone exchange and also the Penn post and sorting office from 1920 until 1988. *Pitlundie* is a substantial house, built in 1913, replacing a house that had burned down. It was occupied by Mrs Becher, the first historian of St Margaret's Church and author of an entertaining memoir of her life in Tylers Green between the wars. A row of old pre-1840 cottages called Widows' Row used to stand behind it. On the other side of the school, *St Enodoc* (1899), of red brick and tile, was built for Mr Cakebread, the gardener of Rayners. *Madryn*, the first of the pair of Edwardian cottages next to *St Enodoc*, was the Penn doctors' surgery from 1960 to 1969.

Pitlundie (EM)

Tylers Green First School - Forster's Education Act of 1870 (introduced under Gladstone's premiership) made the provision of schools for children compulsory for the first time, and a national system of primary schools was established to supplement the existing voluntary schools. In 1874, a headmaster was appointed by the newly-formed Wycombe School Board. For its first two-and-a-half years the school had 95 children on the books, from infants to 13-year-olds, but only 60 or more attending. These were crammed into the former stable block of the mansion house on Elm Road near Widmer Pond, which had been used as an infants' school since 1840.

St Enodoc (JT)

In pouring rain, Philip Rose laid the foundation stone of the new school in October 1875 and it was completed 10 months later. The architect was Arthur Vernon, who later built the Royal Grammar School. He was five times Mayor of Wycombe and was agent for Disraeli's Hughenden Manor estate. In 1896 he became the first man to own a car in Wycombe. The school was built for £1,870 by a Mr Woodbridge of Maidenhead. It is of brick and flint, with tile-hung gables, a central bell tower and separate entrances for boys (right) and girls (left). It had only had two large rooms to start with. The school house on the left was added later and there was a major extension to the right in 1910. Enid Blyton gave out the prizes in 1938. It is a fine building and should be added to the Local List.

Tylers Green First School (EM)

Tylers Green House (JT)

Tylers Green House*, diagonally opposite the school, is also by Vernon. It was built in 1878 as St Margaret's Institute, by Zachariah Wheeler, who had built St Margaret's Church. Sir Philip Rose's purpose was to raise the moral tone of the working classes' by keeping the labouring poor out of the many local pubs. It was designed to be convertible into 'two cottage residences of a superior class' should the venture fail. This is what happened after only 17 years, but it is now one house again. It is much more substantial and ornate than the adjacent vernacular cottages, with walls 18 inches thick, tall chimneys, zigzag brick quoining and tile hanging beneath the upper floor windows. A later owner, Dr Milner, sold off part of the garden on which a pair of houses, 1 & 3 School Road, were built in c. 1965.

Woodbine Cottage (JT)

There is another key grouping of houses in Bank Road as the view opens out facing the school across the common. This is a terrace of five 2-up and 2-down Victorian brick and flint cottages originally named 1-5 Woodbine Cottages (five cigarettes in a workman's 2d packet of Woodbines). They were sold for £55 each in 1887 and are now converted to three houses: *Woodbine Cottage* (c1850), the earliest and central pair, set back from the building line; *Columbine Cottage,* a single cottage to its left (1881, date on side wall); and *Woodbine Corner* (deeds, 1880), a converted pair, which sits on a junction with a green pathway to the Back Common. It has a rendered side-elevation with a small oriel window facing the pathway and a slate roof has been replaced by tiles.

The houses further along, all facing onto the common, surround a large former clay pit. The 1848 Tithe Award describes 15 gardens, but only two cottages, neither of which has survived. The gardens and cottages were all encroachments, but their inclusion on the Tithe map and its description of them as 'gardens' not, as in some other places 'encroachments', gave them a legal basis. Other cottages were built rapidly thereafter, mostly detached, but now with some modern infill. The older buildings are rendered or painted white and cream, and this, with the use of slate roofing, links the buildings.

Columbine Cottage (JT)

Woodbine Corner (JT)

50

Widmer Pond Cottage was built on a plot purchased in 1851 by Zachariah Wheeler for £1.10s. He was to build St Margaret's Church three years later. The new house was sold in 1853 for £35. Prices were rising quite steeply and it was sold in 1875 for £75 and in 1895 for £90. The cottage is set back within its plot and the original very decorative brick and flint, shown in an old photograph has been rendered. The house has been extended to the right and rear. *Hawthorne Cottage* dates from the 1850s or 1860s and has a brick front with decorative dentil eaves and a brick and flint side. It has been extended to the left and rear. The *Bank House* was built in 1936, replacing an earlier brick and flint cottage (sold for £60 in 1935). It is of brick with a semi-rondavel porch and was Barclays Bank from 1936 to 1970 and hence the name of the road. The bank itself occupied only the right half of the ground floor; the remainder housed the manager. It was later converted to two houses and extended to the rear.

Widmer Pond Cottage (JT)

Hawthorne Cottage (JT)

Jasmine Cottage, dates from the 1850s or 60s and once featured in a Kellogg's Corn Flakes advertisement. It has a dominant single stack of brick and has been much extended to the rear. The corner of the road has two new houses on it, *The Ramblers* and *Brambly Hedge,* which replaced the 1860 semi-detached Moulds Villas in 1994. Bank Road then swings to the north where a pair of modern houses, *Tylers Lodge* and *Crabtree Cottage* has replaced a pre-1875 pair of cottages. *Tylers Corner*, now an office, has had an interesting and varied history. In the 1930s it was a cream-painted wooden shed occupied by Jack Busby, one of the four local butchers, and he is remembered killing pigs in his yard. A small brick house was first built in the late 1930s and it was successively a junk shop, a chemist, a ladies hairdresser (Olivia's) from 1964-88, and a carpet shop, with the building steadily growing in size. *Willow Dell* is right in the dell and was built as a bungalow, since extended, on the site of one of two pre-1848 houses. Some of Zachariah Wheeler's descendants live there.

The Bank House (JT)

View across the common to the Red Lion (EM)

Jasmine Cottage (JT)

Tylers Corner (JT)

The Old Bell House (JT)

The Old Bell House* is the earliest and best-documented example of encroachment on both the Wycombe and Penn sides of the common. The encroachment took place in four stages from 1746 to 1781. In 1746, the first plot of land, straddling the parish border, was enclosed and was sold in 1769 to William Turner for £1.11s. 6d. He then built a cottage on an adjacent plot and obtained a licence for a victualling house, to be 'known by the sign of the Bell'. He had to pay an annual rent of one shilling for his encroachment to the lord of the manor. In 1777 and 1781, he enclosed still more land for an orchard. One of the Bassetsbury servants pulled up part of his hedge in a symbolic gesture and Turner had to pay an additional three shillings annual rent. He died intestate in 1783 and by 1795 his son wanted to take over from his reluctant mother.

The family argument ended in 1796 at the summer assizes at Buckingham, and the verdict was a judgement of Solomon splitting the house and land between mother and son.

The present building is in three clearly distinct parts. The oldest part (1769) is the central section. The part to the left was probably built soon after the judge's verdict in 1796. The right-hand section was converted from former Victorian stabling in c.1928. It was a village pub from 1769 until 1922 when it was converted into a house.

View across the Back Common (JT)

Area 5: Back Common

This is a far larger and wilder area than the Front Common, with tracks criss-crossing some 20 acres of grassland, scrub and woodland. There were complaints in 1892 about London boys sent down for a holiday and burning the furze at night. Until the Second World War, the common remained open, almost all gorse, controlled by occasional fires and by grazing animals. The present woodland has grown since then. Football matches used to be played on the open grass and when the weather is right you can still see the lines of the pre- war football pitch.

View across the Back Common (JT)

Cottages to the east of the Back Common (Rays Lane)

Starting at the Village Hall end of Rays Lane - *Acorn Cottage* (pre-1840), originally tiny with bits added at random over the years, presents an array of gables and roof shapes; mostly flint with brick dressings. it also has a cream rendered wing In 1848 it was occupied by Henry Long, a shoe maker, and his wife Esther, a dress-maker. *Blue Gates* was built as a bungalow in 1949 and has been interestingly extended into a chalet-style building with tall chimneys and attractive bargeboards to its dormers. The Travellers Friend, the first beer house

Acorn Cottage (JT)

to be licensed on the common in 1830, was in what is now the back garden. The 1830 Beer Act allowed, for the first time, the sale of beer from premises without a magistrate's licence and within months thousands of beer houses had been opened. Zachariah Wheeler, the builder of St Margaret's Church in 1854, was the publican there in 1848. The beerhouse was demolished together with an adjoining cottage in 1868 and was replaced by The Victoria, now Victoria House, on Elm Road. *Magnolia* (formerly Pollards), a bungalow adjacent to Blue Gates, was built in 1959.

Blue Gates (EM)

The Cottage (EM)

Chepping Cottage (EM)

Graycot (EM)

Rays Yard – the two cottages nearest the track (EM)

Development is more scattered from here on and with larger plots. *The Cottage* is to one side of the rear garden of the Penn Surgery. It is based on a pre-1840 vernacular cottage, larger than the norm, with 3-up and 3-down. In 1848 it was owned and occupied by Frederick Wingrove, a lath mender, born in 1787. He also owned quite a large orchard to the south of the cottage running from Rays Lane up to the main road beside the Horse & Groom. Sir Oliver Millar, former Surveyor of the Queen's Pictures, lives there now..

John Ray (1788-1865) was landlord of The Bell on the Front Common in 1841 and a farrier in 1851. A private census in 1852 shows that the next seven cottages were all owned by him. They were all tiny, 2-up and 2-down, brick and flint, except for the larger 3-up and 2-down *Chepping Cottage,* where he lived himself. It was not there in 1848 and was probably built c.1850 and then extended in 1931. It has an attractive tiled veranda to the front and a small ancillary building of flint under a tile roof. *Graycot*** is one of only three Listed Buildings on the Front or Back Commons. The house sits right at the rear of its plot and has good architectural detailing in its window headers and uses chequered brick. It is on the 1840 map and the date 18Ɛ4 (*sic*) is scratched into the brickwork to the left of the front porch and the initials I.R. in brick are built into the rear flint wall. There was no J in Latin and I was typically used as a substitute, so it presumably stood for John Ray. It has been considerably extended to one side. Its open front garden and that of Chepping Cottage and Rays Yard create a spacious feel in this part of the lane.

Rays Yard** is also Listed. It is now one house, but consists of four tiny cottages set in pairs at right angles to each other creating a courtyard. Four families, three Ray brothers and a Ray daughter, are remembered living there. Each cottage is of a slightly different build and had its own separate roof when first built. Three of them are on the 1840 map. The date 1838 is scratched into the rear wall of the one nearest to the lane, but the two cottages parallel to the lane are thought to be older. In 1852, there was only one privy shared by all four cottages. The cottages are flint with brick dressings under a hipped tiled roof with dentil eaves and pretty casement windows. They are a key feature when turning the corner where the lane diverges. Behind it, on the track to the main road, *Rose Cottage,* another small, pre-1840 vernacular cottage, is the seventh cottage owned by John Ray in 1852. *Elm Cottage*, a post-1840 cottage, originally faced the main road and has been much extended.

Rays yard – the two cottages set back from the track (EM)

Rose Cottage (EM)

Elm Cottage (JT)

Cottages to the north of the Back Common

Fernsdale Cottages, a pair of late Victorian brick and flint cottages, sit close to the road on tiny plots. Both have been nicely extended to the side. *Homeleigh* (plaque,1886), a small neat, brick-built cottage much extended to the rear, overlooks the open common standing on the other side of a track leading down to Potters Cross. Down the track there are two late-Victorian cottages - *Fir Tree Cottage* was a coal yard owned

Fernsdale Cottages (JT)

by George Piggott, who also sawed up large trees for firewood, and *Mistletoe Cottage*. A modern bungalow, *Junipers*, is also are included within the Conservation Area at the top end of the lane. The houses that front the continuation of the track to the west lie outside the boundary, but the manicured strip of green in front of them is retained within it.

Further west, two cottages lie set in woodland. *Heath Cottages,* now one house*,* was formerly a pair built in 1890 (plaque and surveyor's report) by John Saunders, a carman. He ran a haulage business from the yard and kept his horses in the barn there. Decorative brick quoining sets off the flint work of the main frontages, with steep slate roofs and end stacks. Both have been extended to either side. *Gorse Glade* (1931), also of brick, is further along. It was built on a cherry orchard by the son of Thomas Barnes, a successful fruiterer. The orchard used to be called Morley's Orchard after the earlier owner, Luke Morley. *Cherry Cottage* was built by Perfects the builders in 1913, all in brick and not in a vernacular style. It is at the northernmost edge of the Conservation Area close to New Road. Its deeds start with a statutory declaration of 1898 by Henry Saunders, a retired gardener, claiming that he had enclosed the one-fifth-acre of land from the common in 1858.

Homeleigh (JT)

Fir Tree Cottage (EM)

Mistletoe Cottage (EM)

Gorse Glade (JT)

Cherry Cottage (EM)

Heath Cottages (EM)

Nursery Close (JT)

Busby's Nursery Cottage

Church Cottage (JT)

Jubilee Cottage (JT)

Truro Cottage (JT)

Cottages to the south of the Back Common

Nursery Lane. On the southern part of the Back Common, around Nursery Lane, there is an attractive higgledy-piggledly network of tracks, paths and cottages. This group of encroachments surrounds a very large former clay pit with Nursery Lane marking the eastern edge. Most are brick and flint with a varying range in style and appearance, the oldest dating from the 1830s. Some are tucked away down lanes and hidden from wider views. A military map of 1800 shows the lane leading straight from the end of Hammersley Lane to the earliest enclosure on this part of the common where Truro Cottage now stands. The enclosure is bounded by the lane bending to the right and Tickle Belly Alley (see below) to the left. Nursery Lane used to be known as Church Lane until the 1950s, but was popularly called Wizzle Street.

The Parish Room end is dominated by *Nursery Close,* which replaced the *Busby's Nursery* garden and cottage in 1985. Busby's former cottage was a typical brick & flint, 2-up and 2-down, built around 1827, then owned by a tea dealer. Its garden used to be a deep clay pit. At the top end of the lane, two other new houses, *Flintstones* and *Ashdown Cottage,* stand on former nursery ground. *Church Cottage* was two brick and flint cottages known as Church Lane Cottages, which were erected by John Hearn, a bricklayer on a tiny plot in c.1850 on the site of an older cottage which is shown on the 1840 map. He said he had previously 'occupied the land for many years past' and paid £1 for it. The cottages were sold for £60 in 1890. *Jubilee Cottage* appears to have been a two-room bungalow first mentioned in a 1938 sale, apparently created from out-buildings of Church Cottages, to which a first floor was added in c.1960.

Truro Cottage stands on the site of the earliest enclosure on this part of the common, where there seems to have been a house by 1811. The 1848 Tithe Award records a pair of cottages owned and occupied by William Pusey, an agricultural labourer. The present house was built as two cottages in 1884 by Alfred Pusey, a shoemaker from Tyler End Green, Penn. They seem to be an example of an intermediate stage between the flint regarded by the Victorians as cheap and nasty and the more expensive brick, since the exterior walls are an interesting compromise - an inner flint layer and an outer brick skin. The house is set back from the corner of Nursery Lane with a grass path, known to old villagers as Tickle Belly Alley, marking the left hand boundary of the old enclosure. The two cottages were converted into a single house in about 1982.

1 & 2 Nursery Lane. William Hearne, a bricklayer, made a statutory declaration in 1855, claiming that he had sold the plot to his brother Charles, also a bricklayer, in 1850, and that he had owned the land for 19 years before that (i.e. since 1831), and paid £5 for it. He said that he had never paid any quit rent on the land. In other words he made it clear that he had never acknowledged any rights of the lord of the manor. A pair of cottages was built in 1850 and they were sold for £160 in 1914. The present brick and flint house, hidden behind a hedge, was two cottages, but looks later than 1850 and may be a rebuild.

1 & 2 Nursery Lane (EM)

Hope Cottage. In 1875, Zachariah Wheeler (who built St Margaret's Church in 1854), aged 69, made a statutory declaration that he well remembered Moses Ray, a cordwainer (son of John Ray of Rays Lane), fencing in the half-acre in about 1830 and erecting a cottage on it about a year later. Moses Ray was still living there in 1848. By 1875 there were two small cottages facing the common across their large enclosure towards Widmer Pond in the distance. The enclosure was a cherry orchard for over a century, then in the Second World War George Wheeler, a local builder and grandson of Zachariah, had to keep a team of six men for emergency building repairs. There was little bombing in the High Wycombe area and so he set them to work building a factory to make windows and doors. Later occupants were Lucas Industries (1952-82) and then Agropharm, which made fertilisers. The site is now occupied by three modern houses, Barn, Angel and Blackberry Cottages. Hope Cottage is now one house, very considerably extended and rendered.

Hope Cottage (EM)

On the frontage to the Back Common, houses stand in larger, but still randomly sited plots. *Mount Pleasant* (1914, plaque) is built on the site of an earlier building, and is much extended. *Eastleigh is* a small neat Edwardian brick cottage, where Billy Simmonds once mended shoes in an old army hut in the garden. It has since been extended towards the common. It was sold in 1914 for £130. *Isis, Insworth* and *Alma Cottages* formed a terrace of three small cottages facing Tickle Belly Alley and lying at right angles to the main track. A brick above the window at the rear of Alma Cottage has '1838 GR', but there is no one with those initials on the 1841 census return. Isis Cottage was rebuilt in c.1900 after an earlier cottage was burned down. Alma and Insworth Cottages were combined and extended in 1975. They all look out over the huge former claypit behind them.

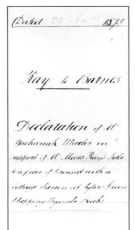

Zachariah Wheeler's Declaration in support of the title to Hope Cottage (Ian Price)

Mount Pleasant (EM)

Isis, Insworth & Alma Cottages (EM)

Eastleigh (EM)

Gorse View and memorial lime trees (JT)

Lost Cottage (JT)

St Anthony's Cottage (EM)

The Parish Room (EM)

The Workshop (JT)

Gorse View was built in 1941 and has the former clay pit in its back garden. *Memorial trees,* planted in c.1920, line the common track, in memory of villagers who died in the First World War. Eight of the original ten survive. They were originally mostly limes marked with the names of those who died, but only one nameplate survives. It is opposite Alma Cottage - E. Bovingdon - whose name is one of 30 on the war memorial on the wall of St Margaret's Church. *Hawthorns* was built in 1959 at the end of a very long garden. *Lost Cottage.* The 1811 map shows a building on the site and there was a substantial house there by 1840. In 1848, it was owned and occupied as one house by Thomas Fawkes who was a sawyer with a wife and three children. It has a brick front and although there is an internal brick and flint timber-framed wall, the timber is used to bond the internal wall not as a structural support for the house. *St Anthony's Cottage,* once called Wee Cot, is also on the 1840 map. It is an attractive small brick and flint cottage that has also been much extended to the rear.

Church Road (East)

The Parish Room was built in 1886 by public subscription for £1,000 on land given by the second Sir Philip Rose. It is flint and red brick with zigzag quoining in the same exuberant style as the school, its bright roof highly visible and enlivened by decorative terracotta ridge tiles. The building is essentially single storey, its steeply pitched roof with a plethora of hipped gable projections and the dark-stained woodwork all make the building stand out on its corner location. A fine central chimney was regrettably removed in 1985. Poverty was still a serious problem when the Parish Room was built and part of it was set aside to be used as a 'Soup Kitchen for the benefit of the Poor inhabitants.' Queen Elizabeth, whom we remember now as the Queen Mother, visited the Parish Room in July 1941, to inspect the WI's jam-making activities as part of the war-time national food production scheme. She pronounced herself thrilled by what she had seen and left with a pot of Bucks stoneless cherry jam to rousing cheers from schoolchildren lining the route.

In 1935 the trustees were seriously investigating the possibility of demolishing the Parish Room and putting up a new building, but decided that the area could support a separate village hall. This was built the following year and the trustees then agreed to resign and hand over the Parish Room to the Vicar and Churchwardens of St Margaret's Church. A large extension with stained-glass memorial windows was added to the Parish Room in 1995.

The Workshop buildings on the opposite corner were originally a simple weather-boarded structure used as a carpenter's shop and store for the Rose estate. It is now offices and has been extended into the roof by four large dormers.

Crossways, next to the Parish Room, is a two-storey early 20th-century house (it is on the 1923 map) with gables and dormers breaking up the front elevation. It is now used as an office. *Barn, Angel* and *Blackberry Cottages* are a new 1996 housing development on a former factory site. They are a mix of brick, flint and weatherboarding, considerably larger than vernacular cottages, and line the side of a small green, dominated by car parking on the frontages. with a fine red chestnut tree planted by the WI to celebrate George V's Jubilee in 1935.

Crossways (JT)

Bowyers/Gorse View, to the north of the green, is on another island encroachment backing on to a former clay pit which was used as the village rubbish dump and known as Clutterdell, in use until an effective council refuse collection service was established in the 1950s. It is an Edwardian brick house, rendered, with a tiled roof, and was built by George Wheeler in 1908 for £203. It was formerly (1961-75) Bowyer's grocer's shop and now sells office furniture. An attractive coursed-flint outbuilding is adjacent.

Barn, Angel and Blackberry Cottages (EM)

Heathside, next to Bowyers, is the only identified site of a 'Turf House', which is presumably what Philip Rose was thinking of when he was writing about 'mud houses' being built during the early settlement of the common. In the parish box in the diocesan record office in Oxford there is a scrap of paper recording an agreement in November 1849 between Thomas Fowler (see *Tyler End*) and James Menday (with a very shaky signature) for the sale of a piece of ground and 'the Turf House on the said Garden…situate at Tylers Green near the Gravel Pitts…with all the contents and the water courses'. James Menday was paid £1.5s. The 1848 Tithe map shows him owning and occupying a cottage and garden on this site and the 1841 census shows that he was an agricultural labourer, then about 55 years old, apparently living in the same place with his wife, two grown-up children and a grandchild.

Gorse View (Bowyers) (JT)

Thomas Fowler died in 1856 and his will refers to this same piece of land, but without mention of the turf house which he had presumably removed. The present house was later owned, occupied and probably built by Thomas Barnes, a very successful fruiterer, whose will in 1913 shows that he owned 14 cottages, six detached and four pairs. They included Eastleigh, and 1 & 2 Nursery Cottages in Nursery Lane. He had earlier owned Busby's Nursery (now Nursery Close). He also owned seven orchards known by evocative names such as Whipping Toms (now 31 New Road), Morley's Orchard (now Gorse Glade), and Black Orchard (thought to be the orchard opposite Rays Yard and Graycot and referring to black cherries). These were then all cherry orchards from which Thomas Barnes produced over £600 of annual sales to the Bristol Fruit Market. Heathside was sold in 1914 for £392 and has since been considerably extended.

Heathside (JT)

Little Barn, on the corner of Bank Road, is a c. 1930 house of white render with brick detailing. It can be seen in the background of the photograph when the red horse chestnut tree was planted on the green in 1935 to celebrate George V's Jubilee.

W.I. planting red chestnut tree in 1935 with Little Barn in the background

The Village Hall (EM)

The *Village Hall* was built the following year, by George Wheeler, in the garden cherry orchard next to the Fox & Pheasant pub, for a cost of £2,150 raised by public subscription. A kitchen was added to the rear in 1951 and it was extended to one side in 1980 and refronted, as a Millennium project, in 2000. It sits well back, with car parking to the front and an open grass space to one side where the pub used to stand. The Fox & Pheasant had closed in 1914 when George Slade the landlord had been called up. On his return he became a coal merchant and his wife sold sweets. He moved his coal-merchant business to a new house by Widmer Pond, now called Merchants Yard.

Church View, Spring Cottage and Rosepatch Cottage (JT)

Opposite, there is a terrace of low vernacular cottages with large porches; *Church View*, which turns the corner, is unpainted roughcast, taller than the adjacent *Spring Cottage* and *Rosepatch Cottage,* but all three were originally three tiny post-1848, 2-up and 2-down cottages. The two end-cottages have been extended and the roof of Church View was raised in c.1950. *Kingsgate,* originally a 1961 bungalow, marks the start of the open common.

1 & 2 Cherry Tree Cottage, looking out over the Back Common, are based on a small, mid-Victorian pair of cottages, which by 1947 had become a grocer's and a television and radio shop/general store. In 1956 they were converted to domestic use and have been considerably extended on both sides, with a mixture of render and paint under a shallow slate roof. The recently-closed *pharmacy/post office* is a modern building which was the last post office in the village from 1989 to 2004. A track to one side leads into the now abandoned *Hazlemere Upholstery* factory in a former clay pit. The site remained largely an orchard until 1952 when George Wheeler set up a joinery factory making windows and doors. Hazlemere Upholstery followed, making and upholstering chairs, until 2005. Planning permission has recently been given for three private houses. Opposite is the *Old Horology Shop* (c.1900), once a shoe shop, then a clock shop, which although now a house still retains its shop front. It has a large tile motif (that has no relation to Penn tiles) on the upper storey. It looks out both over the common and over another small green.

1 & 2 Cherry Tree Cottage (JT)

Small green showing former pharmacy and post office (EM)

The Old Horology Shop (JT)

60

Pippins Cottage (1850, deeds), a small early-Victorian brick and flint cottage facing on to the small green, is set back, hidden by hedges and trees with only its upper floor and tiled roof visible through the gated gap in the hedge. It was sold for £180 in 1904 and has since been much extended. On the south side of the green three modern bungalows, *Nutwith Cottage, Cherry Dale* and *Tylers Dell*, have been attractively extended. To the north, *Wheelers,* originally a pre-1840 vernacular cottage, (owned by William Wheeler, a common dealer, in 1848), has now been greatly extended into flats for the elderly. *Cypress Cottage* was built in 1963 in part of the orchard of The Old Bell House by Mr Blacklaw, the last manager of Barclays Bank in Bank Road.

Pippins Cottage (EM)

Bethlehelm Meeting Hall. In 1839, Robert Wingrove, a labourer from Tyler End Green, applied for a meeting house licence for the Primitive Methodists and one of their earliest chapels was built, in 1840, to serve both parishes at a cost of £174. It was known as the Rehoboth Chapel but was known locally as the 'Little Rarnters'. The Primitive Methodists were seeking to revive the fervour of early Methodism and held open air revivals known as 'camp meetings', one of which at Penn, presumably on the common, attracted 1,500 people, 'many of whom were pricked in their hearts'. It is now used by an independent religious group. The building has two white-painted gables, the earlier brick and flint on the right and a similar-sized brick extension (c.1920) on the left, both with shallow slate roofs.

Wheelers flats (EM)

At the end of Church Road, a tiny pre-1840 cottage, appropriately known as *The Dolls House,* shares the same courtyard as the estate agents Jackson Howes. Their building was formerly Streeter's (and earlier, Clarke's), the butcher's shop and there was a slaughter house in the courtyard. The Dolls House is of quite fancy brickwork and both its sides are brick rather than flint. There were already 'premises' here in 1796, marked on a sketch map attached to the report of a legal case concerning The Old Bell House. It may have been the presence of these premises which decided the direction of Church Road (East) from the end of Hammersley Lane.

Bethlehem Meeting Hall (EM)

Church Road (West)

Church Road (West) presents a very different picture because its southern side has never been common land and so is the home of more 'respectable' dwellings than the common. They are not encroachments and so are grander and rather earlier - the 1761 Rocque map shows houses already lining the southern edge of the road. The houses are mostly built of brick rather than brick and flint which was so despised by the Victorians and many are detached and on larger plots. Former glebe property along the stretch of road below the church includes three Listed Buildings, Tyler Cottage, Tyler End, and opposite, Dell Cottage. There is a particularly attractive view down to the Horse & Jockey, sitting in the dip.

The Dolls House (EM)

St Margaret's Church (EM)

St Margaret's Church (EM)

St Margaret's Church (JT)

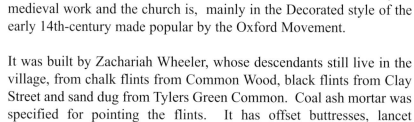

View up from near the Horse & Jockey (JT)

St Margaret's Church. ** Although the church is prominent in the immediate locality, it was a late arrival and the village did not grow up around it. The first Earl Howe gave 'a small piece of meadow land fronting the Green', the site of an old brick kiln, with a cottage occupied by the aptly named John Priest. The cottage had to be dismantled to make way for the church, which was built in 1854, thanks to the energy and money of Sir Philip Rose, and was named after his wife. It was designed by David Brandon, a young Jewish architect, who had just been awarded a medal for his work on the Great Exhibition of 1851, and went on to be vice-president of the RIBA. He had made a study of medieval work and the church is, mainly in the Decorated style of the early 14th-century made popular by the Oxford Movement.

It was built by Zachariah Wheeler, whose descendants still live in the village, from chalk flints from Common Wood, black flints from Clay Street and sand dug from Tylers Green Common. Coal ash mortar was specified for pointing the flints. It has offset buttresses, lancet windows and an unusual detached wooden bell-cote, designed by Arthur Vernon, which was erected, in 1889, again by Zachariah Wheeler, in memory of Sir Philip Rose's wife. A 1932 extension created a longer sanctuary with a new south window, and a new round window replacing the traditional stained-glass east window. John Betjeman described the interior as 'rather striking'. The Rose family; Sir Arthur Whitten Brown, the first man to fly the Atlantic (with Sir John Alcock); Elizabeth Russell, the novelist; her brother Sir Sydney Beauchamp; and Walter de la Mare's wife are all buried there. The long brick and flint boundary wall was built by local builders for only £90.

The *Old Queen's Head*** first appears in deeds of 1666, called Bushes, when it was purchased by Martin Lluelyn, one of Charles II's physicians, who was Mayor of Wycombe in 1671. He was married to a descendant of the Puttenham family. It may have been a small farm and it still had 5½ acres in 1800 when it became a Wethereds public house, owning all the land to the north including the site of the present First School. It has a former barn on the left side with timber-framed elements, dated 1666, still shown separate from the main building on the 1840 map. The main building dates from two periods: c.1800, which was the time when Wycombe's furniture industry

The Old Queen's Head (EM)

had just started to attract a new labour force; and from 1854 when an extension was built, presumably in anticipation of custom from the new church, built that same year. It has some remnant internal timber-framing and is mostly cream-painted render. One of the Edwardian landlords went by the memorable name of Alphabet Brown.

Beechwood, opposite the church, is a larger than usual brick and flint house. 'K.H.1877' can be seen on a plaque at ground level, to the right of the front door. It was extended in 1976.

Beechwood (JT)

Tyler Cottage**, below the church, was left in a will of 1810 by Mary Morris, wife of the farmer at Puttenham Place, to her nephew Thomas Hearne of Pennbury Farm. It was described as a cottage. It is not on a map of 1800. When it was sold in 1846 to Philip Rose for £105, it had been occupied for many years by Charlotte Weller the daughter of Mary Morris and wife of Thomas Weller, a butcher and second son of the Amersham brewing family (see page 30). In 1846 the house sat in a garden of just over an acre extending into the present graveyard. It was used as a school room from 1846 and for some church services prior to the construction of St Margaret's. Philip Rose gave the cottage towards the endowment for the new Vicar and a large part of the garden to add to the graveyard. The house has defined architectural characteristics such as a band course and dentil eaves. Built of brick with a hipped tile roof, it has a blocked central doorway with sundial above and a half spiral staircase. It has a brick and flint timber-framed wall inside, but the timber is used to bond the internal wall not as a structural support for the house. It was sold by the vicar in 1919 and has recently been extended.

Tyler Cottage (EM)

Tyler End** is a fine two-storey flint house with particularly good gothic windows on its upper floor and a tiled roof. It dates from approximately 1819 when John Hearne, a husbandman of Penn Street, took out a mortgage for £120. The rear wing is late 19th-century. In 1823 it was described as 'messuage now used as two tenements'. In 1849, it was purchased by Thomas Fowler, 'a proprietor of houses'. Thomas Fowler (1790-1856) was a very successful Methodist 'immigrant' from Kingsey and Haddenham, who in 1818 was a butcher in Penn, but when he made his will could describe himself as a gentleman and was a wealthy man with several properties. The Tyler End property included several acres, three cottages and a bakehouse,

Tyler End (EM)

Dell Cottage (EM)

Dell Cottage (Trevor Price)

Looking down towards the Horse & Jockey (JT)

The Horse & Jockey (JT)

The Laurels (JT)

probably used by one of his sons who was a baker. It is likely that Thomas Fowler made the house into what we see today. After his death, the property was sold to the first Earl Howe who gave the house, its adjoining cottage, bakehouse and nearly five acres of garden, orchard and meadow, valued at £700, as an endowment for the vicar of St Margaret's. It is tucked away from public view and surrounded by the newer development of Glebelands in its former garden. It used to be called Ivy Cottage and the vicar, the Rev. Ashley Spencer, lived there during the First World War. His successor sold it in 1919.

Dell Cottage**, set far back in its plot to the north of Church Road, is one of only three Listed Buildings on the common itself. When sold in 1919, there were 'two old-fashioned cottages' with 1½ acres and a gate to the Back Common. In 1868, Harry Hawes, a labourer, aged 85 (so born in 1783), made a statutory declaration which is a good example of its kind.

"I Harry Hawes of Tylers Green, labourer, do solemnly swear as follows: That I am of the age of 85 years & upwards. That I have resided all my life in or near Tylers Green….and consequently....well acquainted with …properties…tenants. That the land or ground which now forms the site of the three cottages and gardens at Tyler's Green now occupied by….and the adjoining Orchard & Pasture Land more particularly known as "the Dell" now in the occupation of…..were for a long time prior to 1810 the properties of Mr Thomas Weller of Penn, Butcher who sold them in 1810…That I distinctly remember the two cottages now occupied by….being built by Thomas Weller. That I also remember that between 70 and 80 years ago there were two old cottages standing in the bottom of "the Dell" both of which have since been pulled down and removed….

If the two old cottages in the dell, which were still there in 1848 but had gone by 1868, were built, as claimed, between 1788 and 1798, they are the earliest recorded encroachment after the Old Bell House. The origin of the cottage we see today is recorded in an 1803 conveyance of 'two freehold cottages lately now erected and built adjoining together at or near Tyler End Green and nearly facing the brick kiln there.' Thomas Weller didn't build the cottages, as remembered by Harry Hawes, but paid £90 for them, together with 1.5 acres and 'common of pasture and other rights of common'. In 1871, the second Earl Howe added the cottages and land, valued at £300, to St Margaret's endowment. A third cottage had been built to one side of the pair at some stage, but had gone when it was sold by the vicar in 1919. It is now one house, solidly built with 13 inch brick walls on the ground floor and standing on very large sandstones. The decorative chequer brickwork indicates a higher status building.

The *Horse and Jockey** (1837, mortgage), first licensed in 1844, by Wellers the Amersham Brewers, as the Horse & Groom, and so-called for many years despite its older rival on Elm Road, sits in a dip below St Margaret's Church. It is a small public house of three bays with a yellow rendered front and flint side walls with brick dressings. It is aligned sideways to the road and faces Tyler Cottage on the other side of the dip. A small treed area of drive to the front, with a track that used to lead to Ashwells Farm, provides the setting for the building and it creates an attractive pinch point to the street scene. Wellers sold to Benskins in 1930. The elevated brick and flint frontage of *The Laurels* (1848, in brickwork by front door) is on the other side of the road, and its attractive outbuilding of flint sits hard by the road.

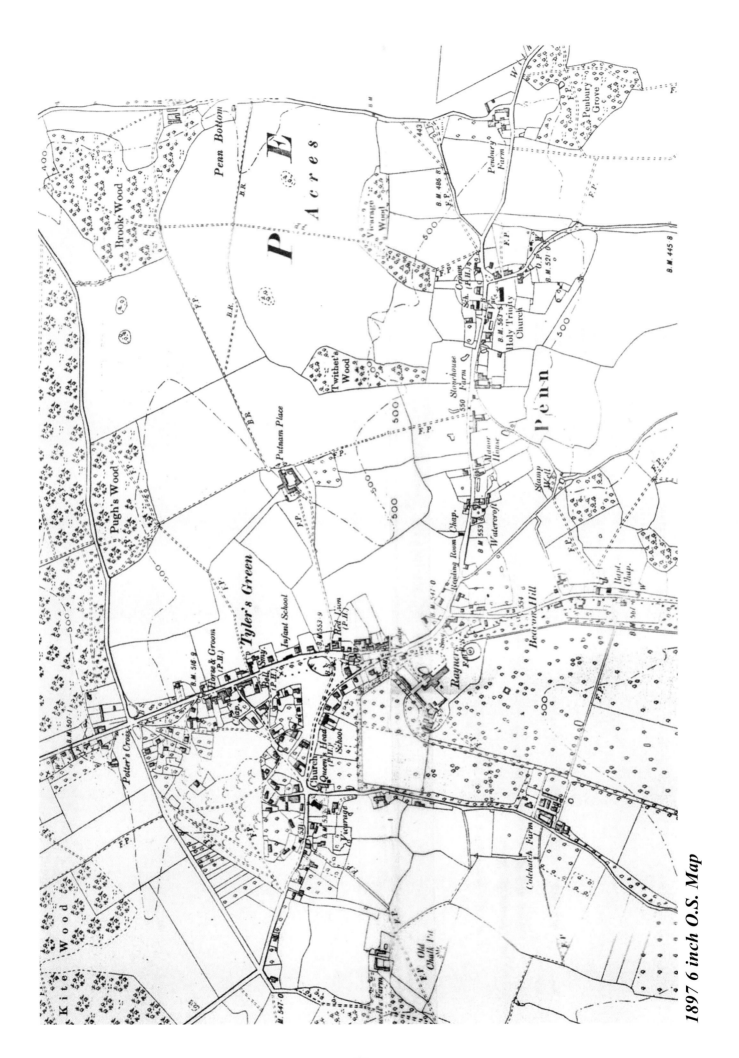

1897 6 inch O.S. Map

65

The Old Rectory (EM)

The White House (EM)

Open ride marking edge of common and former boundary of St John's Wood (JT)

White House Cottage and White Rose Cottage (JT)

View towards St Margaret's Church (JT)

The Old Rectory**, 'lately erected' in 1838, is a surprise with its formal and precise lines at complete odds with the vernacular cottages of the encroachments. Set well back from the road within a wide plot, the front of the building is colour-washed render, the rear being of humbler flint with brick dressings. The entrance wings are set back from the main front and the symmetrical appearance of the whole, within its lawned grounds, tall windows, and well-proportioned rooms, resembles the grand stuccoed Regency villas in Penn, described earlier. Actually, it was built as a superior pair of semi-detached cottages, Caroline and Compton Cottages, set in ³/₄ acre, and first occupied by a Dissenting minister and a land surveyor. They replaced an earlier cottage. It was one of only two houses which were given a name in the 1841 census for Tylers Green. Philip Rose considered, but rejected, their conversion into one house for the vicarage of St Margaret's, and in 1871 Earl Howe gave the two cottages, valued at £700, to St Margaret's for an endowment. The Vicar had them converted into one house in 1885, renamed as The Firs, and was soon complaining that his tenant was asking for an inside WC. A later vicar, the Rev. Gerald Hayward, lived there after the First World War for a few years and returned in the 1940s. His successor lived there for 10 years until 1961, when a new vicarage was built and The Firs was sold. It was a parsonage rather than a rectory.

The White House is a substantial mid-Victorian residence (now divided into three) overlooking an open stretch of common planted with some fine beech trees. It is a stuccoed house in Italianate style with three hipped protruding gables, and has elegantly-proportioned sash windows and broad-bracketed eaves. It was built in 1875 by James Wight, a builder (hence it was called the Wight House), and was extended in 1926 when a library wing was added to the west. Bateman Lancaster Rose, brother of the second Sir Philip Rose, lived there from 1903 and his widow was there until the mid-1950s. She was a very 'grande dame' and was driving down to Beaconsfield one day when she was stopped by a tramp who asked for a lift saying 'the Lord told me to stop your car.' He got into the car, but Mrs Lancaster Rose soon realised that she had made a mistake and said to him, 'The Lord told you to stop my car for you to get in, but now he has told me to stop it for you to get out!' The present baronet, Sir David Rose, is the grandson of Lancaster Rose and was brought up there. Veronica Papworth, the journalist, divided the house into three in the early 1960s (the newer library wing is now No 3).

The butler and chauffeur lived in the older adjoining *White House Cottage* and *White Rose Cottage*. Both are white-rendered with decorative ridge tiles. They are the only survivors of a group of five cottages shown on the 1848 Tithe map and may have earlier belonged to Ashwells Farm whose deeds indicate a pre-1787 date. In 1907 they were sold as a pair with long gardens at the rear by Dr William Rose of Ashwells to his cousin Lancaster Rose for £470. Their plots mark the western end of the Conservation Area right at the edge of the former St John's Wood and White Rose Cottage was then appropriately called Woodview. White House Cottage was Fern Cottage.

There is a fine view looking back towards the church. It is the many open spaces, small greens and lack of any overall design which gives the common and its surrounds a particular charm. A miscellany of buildings of all ages stands on plots of all sizes, linked by roads and tracks that have no apparent pattern. It is the very antithesis of town planning. Growth has been organic, and both the buildings and their setting, when properly interpreted, tell the story of the preceding centuries

Dutch gables on Pewsey Cottage (JT)

Peculiar local details

<u>Dutch gables</u> - in brick are found on *Pewsey Cottage* and *Old Bank House*, both of which are thought to have been lodges to Puttenham Place. They are rather late examples of a style that was popular from the 1630s. The motif has been picked up in brick and flint on later buildings; *Chestnuts* and *Snowdrop Cottage (Collaine)*, the pair of estate cottages on Elm Road, built in 1848 by Earl Howe and *The Old Laundry*, built by Sir Philip Rose, probably a year later. *Penn Ridge*, on Church Road, Penn, near Pewsey Cottage, built in c.1913, makes a nod in the same direction.

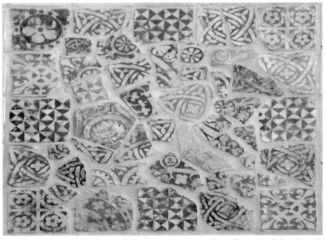

Mosaic of medieval Penn tiles on the floor of the Lady Chapel in Penn Church (EM)

<u>Penn floor tiles.</u> Original 14th-century Penn tiles can be seen in the Lady Chapel of *Penn Church*. Larger Victorian tiles decorate the gate pillars to *Rayners* and the house itself, and the former *Old Horology Shop* in Church Road (East).

<u>Caricature of Gladstone</u>. A clay caricature stands on the ridge of *The Elms*, facing the Front Common on Elm Road, which apparently came from Rayners where Sir Philip Rose was demonstrating his support for his friend Disraeli who was Gladstone's arch political rival.

Caricature of Gladstone (EM)

Traditional building materials

Brick was not used at all until the 14th-century and then only for particularly important buildings. Almost all the buildings in Penn up to the 17th-century would have been of wattle and daub with a timber frame. Clay tiles were made locally from at least 1222, but it is probable that only the bigger buildings would have had a tiled roof, with the majority thatched. Wooden shutters would have covered the few window spaces, hardly any of which would have been glazed. The few surviving timber-framed buildings have replaced their exterior wattle and daub with a brick infill between the timbers.

Timber-framing on Church & Crown Cottage (EM)

By the 18th-century, brick was being widely used, but timber-framing could survive into the early 19th-century for ordinary cottages. In 1822, William Cobbett riding from Chesham to Wycombe described the labourers' dwellings as good, 'being constructed of brick-nog, which he described as a frame of wood with a single brick filling and covered with tile. No evidence of brick-nog has been noted in the Conservation Area. Today's highly prized old brick and flint cottages are nearly all 19th-century and cease abruptly with the First World War in 1914, after which the cost of labour made them uneconomical.

The buildings in the Conservation Area exhibit the full range of traditional Chiltern materials, both on grand houses and humble cottages. They are a useful indicator not only of how building types and styles developed over the course of time, but also of the historical development of the settlement pattern. Building materials tie together diverse groups of buildings.

<u>Timber-framing</u> can still be seen on older buildings with brick infill panels, but the fashion for re-facing the fronts of older buildings in more expensive brick has meant that it is usually only visible at the rear or internally. *Church Cottage*, opposite the Crown, *Stratfords Cottage* opposite Slades Garage, and the *Old Queen's Head barn*, are examples where timber-framing is readily visible.

Stucco on The Old Rectory (EM)

<u>Stucco and render</u>. - Stucco, a plaster of lime and fine sand with oil, became fashionable during the Georgian and Regency periods to provide a smooth cover and is seen on the grander buildings. *The Old Vicarage, South View, Stonehouse* and *Watercroft* are all rendered in stucco. The practice trickled down to smaller buildings, such as *Penn Cottage*, and the upper floor of *Cotters Barn*. Later buildings also used stucco – *The Old Rectory* and *The White House* in Tylers Green are examples of smaller dwellings being given the grand treatment.

<u>Local brick</u> was used as facing material on polite buildings and vernacular cottages. It has been used to great decorative effect, for example, on houses such as *The Knoll*, where the use of brick indicates a high-status building for its period, on the *Troutwells* group, and on the former *lodges to Puttenham Place*. *Yonder Lodge* and *French Meadow* are of brick, colourwashed. Brick is also used for architectural detailing: *1-3 Paul's Hill* have brick drip-moulds over the windows, and many older buildings have brick stringcourses and eaves details, the group of *Dilehurst* and *Kings* being a good example. Decoratively different types of brick are used for window headers, for decorative Dutch gables, and for chequer work on houses such as *Dell Cottage* opposite St Margaret's Church. *April Cottage* in Elm Road uses red

Red brick with purple headers on April Cottage (EM)

brick with purple headers to good effect. As brick became more widely available, many Victorian buildings had brick as their main material, if it could be afforded, and humbler dwellings had their fronts refaced.

Mortar The type of mortar used can also have a decorative impact. At *Cobblers, Wren Cottage, Chapel Cottage* and *The Red House*, pale lime render sets off the bricks to great effect.

Imported bricks began to be utilised by the middle of the 19th-century, identifiable by their colour. Thus *Penn Church Hall*, then a school, was built for

Pale yellow London brick used on the Jackson Howes building (EM)

Earl Howe by a fashionable architect, in 1839, in pale yellow London stock. They were also used for the extension of the *Free Methodist Chapel* in 1875. The late Victorian, former butcher's shop, now occupied by *Jackson Howes,* uses yellow bricks in decorative bands to great effect.

Flint is the only local building stone, apart from the large sarsen stones sometimes used as foundation stones on the oldest buildings. Because flint was both cheap and readily available, it was widely used on a range of buildings, but we have already noted that the Victorians despised flint work, and at the very least looked for a 'respectable' brick front. *Penn Church* is mainly of flint because there was no concept of bricks when it was built. *St Margaret's Church* is mainly flint, because it is deliberately copying the Gothic period, but it may be that the ivy, shown in early photographs as completely covering the walls of the church, was a later Victorian attempt to conceal the flintwork. The examples of high Victoriana, such as the *Parish Rooms, Tylers Green School* and *St. Margaret's Institute* (now Tylers Green House) use flint very decoratively, with diagonal brickwork quoins.

Tylers Green House (EM)

Flint and flint with brick dressings is very common on the smaller cottages of the encroachments and elsewhere in the later settlement. The *Penn Estate cottages* on Elm Road, and even a small hut in St Margaret's churchyard, show how versatile and decorative the material can be. Flint is also used throughout the Conservation Area on boundary walls.

Flintwork on the hut in St Margaret's graveyard (JT)

Early use of Welsh slate used on The Old Vicarage (JT)

Welsh slate was used on some grander villas, such as the *Old Vicarage* and *South View*, from the early 19th-century, allowing a shallower roof pitch in the classical style. Its use may have been encouraged by the Brick Tax on bricks and tiles, first imposed in 1784 to defray the cost of the American War of Independence, and continued until 1833. Slate became more widely available and cheaper during the 19th-century, particularly after the railway arrived in Wycombe in 1854, and was then used on more of the Victorian cottages. It was appreciated as a better means of collecting drinkable rainwater because it was less absorbent than clay tile and grew less moss.

Weatherboarding on the Old Queen's Head (EM)

Weatherboarding tends to be used on functional buildings such as barns and outbuildings, often a reminder of a more rural past. Both *Penn Barn* and the *Yonder Lodge* barn have white weatherboarded elevations. Traditional dark-stained weatherboarding can be seen on former agricultural buildings and outbuildings such as: the granary at *Grove's Barn*, the barns at *King's,* and the *Old Queen's Head* and the *Workshop* buildings opposite. Weatherboarding has also been used on the new housing development of *Barn, Angel* and *Blackberry Cottages*. Although widely spread, these buildings help tie parts of the Conservation Area together and hark back to a more rural past.

The Natural Features Map

The *Natural Features Map* (inside back cover) identifies the open spaces, views, trees, hedges, walls and ponds that are considered particularly important to the character of the Conservation Area.

Trees are fundamental to the rural character of the area. At *Penn Church*, the lime trees along the front boundary are fine specimens, planted c.1850. Other good specimens are seen along the road towards Tylers Green, particularly around *Long Pond* in front of Stone House Grange, and at *Lane House*. *Beacon Hill* has a sylvan feel due to the many mature trees that shade the area.

Three lime trees by Widmer Pond (JT)

The Front Common. There are two oaks near the bus stop: the smaller and heavily pruned one was planted to commemorate the 1935 Silver Jubilee; the larger one commemorates the present Queen's coronation in 1953 – Harold Wheeler's daughter Marion remembers helping plant it as a young girl.

In 1960, when it was obvious that the century-old elm trees lining Elm Road were on their last legs, a row of oaks, originally 12, but apparently with later replanting, were planted below *Widmer Pond*. The members of Penn Parish Council each contributed a tree. The three large lime trees close to Widmer Pond look about the same age.

In 1979, to belatedly mark the present Queen's Silver Jubilee: 12 small-leafed limes were planted to form a parallel row with the established row of oaks, with a group of four Italian alders at the pond end; a large-leafed lime was placed outside Laundry Cottages; and three more Italian alders were put on the common opposite the First School. In 1985, four wych elms, a species particularly resistant to Dutch Elm disease, were planted on the far verge of Elm Road opposite the pond.

Trees on the Front Common (JT)

The small green opposite the Village Hall has a red chestnut planted by the WI in 1935, also to celebrate the Jubilee of George V, and two fine later, but well-established, copper beeches.

On the *Back Common*, there is a memorial row of trees lining the track past Bowyers which were planted c.1920, in memory of the men who died in the First World War. There are 30 names on the war memorial on the south wall of St Margaret's Church. There are eight surviving trees, lime and beech, with two gaps. The trees are planted at a uniform distance of 15 paces. Each of the ten trees presumably represented three men. Only one name plate survives - at the foot of a lime tree opposite Alma Cottage – to E. Bovingdon and this corresponds to Ernest Bovingdon on the war memorial. The trees are well-established and would make a long and impressive row if the scrub around the lower half was cleared away. Opposite the Old Rectory, there are other fine mature specimens of beech and copper beech set within mown grassland.

The row of memorial limes on the Back Common (JT)

Historical Maps:

The following maps were used to determine the development of the settlement over time. Those with an asterisk have been included in this book:

*1761, Rocque
1766, Jeffery
1777, Andrews & Drury, 25 miles around Windsor
*1800, Military map (horseback)
1811, 2 inch O.S. survey
1822, 1 inch O.S.
1824, Bryant
1836, St John's Wood
1838, Penn Tithe
*1840, Chepping Wycombe parish map
1848, Wycombe Tithe
*1852, Penn Inclosure map B
*1863, St Margaret's District
*1875, 25 inch O.S.
*1897, 25 inch O.S.
*1897, 6 inch O.S.
*1912, Little Domesday map, Penn
1923/38, 6 inch O.S.
1925, 25 inch O.S.
*2006, Jo Tiddy's three maps of the Conservation Area are based on an up-to-date O.S. map.

Bibliography

Victoria County History, Bucks, III (1925)

PEVSNER, Nikolaus and WILLIAMSON, Elizabeth, *The Buildings of England, Buckinghamshire* Penguin (1994)

WILLIAMSON E, An *inventory of the Historic Monuments of Buckinghamshire*, RCHM (1912)

GREEN, Miles and CLARK, Evelyn, *The Rose Family, Rayners and Tyler's End Green*, Locally published (1982)

GREEN, Miles, *The history of St Margaret's Church*, Tyler's Green, Locally published (1984)

GREEN, Miles and SHARP, Pat, *The diary of Daniel Baker 1690-1705*, Locally published (1999)

GREEN, Miles, HUNT, Barbara and TEBBUTT, Liz, *Penn & Tylers Green in Old Photographs*, Sutton (2000)

GREEN, Miles, *Medieval Penn floor tiles*, Locally published (2003)

GREEN, Miles, *A potted history of Penn & Tylers Green*, Unpublished (2005)

GREEN, Miles, *The illegal settlement of Tylers Green Common*, Unpublished (2005)

Index

Elm Cottage, Three, 36, 54
Elm Road, 5, 6, 29, 30, 34, 35, 37, 40, 42, 44, 49, 71
Elmside, 34
Elms, The, 2, 34, 67
Emily's Cottage, 32
Enclosures, see Inclosure Award
Encroachers, 5, 42, 44, 52
Evans, Walter, 24
Fawkes, Thomas, 58
Fern Cottage, 66
Fernsdale Cottages, 55
Field House, 23
Firs, The, 66
Fir Tree Cottage, 55
Flexman, John, 16
Flintstones, 56
Fowler, Thomas, 29, 59, 63, 64
Fox & Pheasant, 60
Fox, George, 34
France, fall of in 1940, 9
Fraser, Antonia, 16
French House Mead, 35
French Meadow, 36, 37, 68
French School, 6, 35, 40
Front Common, 3, 5, 6, 32, 33, 35, 42, 48, 53, 54, 71

Gable Cottage, 29, 30
Garland, Charles, 22
Garland family, 10
Garlands, carpenters, 16
Garret Green, 19, 42
George III, King, 14
George V, King, 18, 59, 71
German invasion feared, 9
Gerrards Green, 42
Gladstone, William, Prime Minister; 34, 48, 67;   clay caricature, 2, 34, 67
Glebelands, 64
Glenmore, 26
Gorse Glade, 55
Gorse View, 58
Granary, The, 32
Grasside, 22
Graycot, 54, 59
Great Exhibition, 1851, 62
Great Northern Railway, 27
Great Widmore Pond, 35
Green Belt, 5
Green Farm, 36
Greenhurst, 37
Griffen, Mr, builder, 36
Grove Cottage, 15
Grove, Edmund, 14
Grove family, 14, 15, 16
Grove, George, 14
Grove, John, 12, 16
Grove, Sir George, 16
Grove's Barn, 15, 16, 17
Guest, Keen & Nettlefolds (GKN), 18
Guinness, company, 11

Hall, Laurence, 16
Hamilton House, 48
Hammersley, 42
Hammersley Lane, 27, 42, 56
Hampdens, 24, 26

Hancock family, 26
Harrison-Townsend, Mr, 12
Harrow-on-the-Hill, 36
Hatchetts Mead, 11
Hatchits, 11
Haviland, General, 35
Hawes, Harry, 64
Hawthorne Cottage, 51
Hawthorns, 58
Hayward, Rev. Gerald, 66
Hazlemere, 46
Hazlemere Road, 44, 46
Hazlemere Upholstery, 60
Heal, Mrs Ralph, 12
Helmore, Sir James, 23
Henry VIII, King, 15, 33
Hearne, Charles, 57
Hearne, John, 56, 63
Hearne, Thomas, 63
Hearne, William, 57
Heath Cottages, 55
Heath End, 42
Heathside, 59
Heath, Sir Barrie, 18
High Wycombe, 3, 5, 16, 18, 27, 42, 48, 57, 68, 70
Hillbrow Cottage, 16
Hillcrest Cottage, 40
Hitler, Adolf, 14
Holiness Mission, 36
Holmore Wood, 16
Holy Trinity Church, Penn, 3, 5, 6, 8, 10, 18, 22, 24, 34, 35, 67, 69, 71
Holy Trinity Church, Penn Street, 22
Home Guard, 9, 11, 28
Homeleigh, 55
Hoover, Herbert, President, 36
Hope Cottage, 57
Horse & Groom, 40, 54
Horse & Jockey, 5, 61, 62, 64
Houses, prices contrasted 1854/today, 46
Howe, Countess: wife of 1st Earl, 12
Howe, Countess: divorced first wife of the 5th Earl, 11
Howe, Dowager Countess : widow of 5th Earl, his third wife, 21
Howe, 1st Earl, 12, 22, 36, 44, 62, 64, 66
Howe, 2nd Earl, 22, 64
Howe, 5th Earl, 11
Howe, 7th Earl, 34
Hughenden Manor, 27, 28, 49

Ideal Home Exhibition 1927, 11
Ilbert, Sir Courtenay Peregrine, 15
Inclosure Award, Penn 1855, 35
Inclosure Award, St John's Wood, 1868, 46
Ivy Cottage, 15, 64
Insworth Cottage, 57
Isis Cottage, 57

Jackson Howes, 40, 42, 61, 69
Japonica, 36
Jasmine Cottage, 51
Jollye, Betty, 3, 11
Jollye, Lt. S.A., 11

Jubilee Cottage, 56
Jubilee of King George V, 59, 71
Jubilee of Queen Elizabeth II, 71
Junipers, 55

Keld Cottage, 21
Kellogg's Corn Flakes, 51
Kenilworth, 36
Kilns, site of, 37
King's barn, 30
King's, butchers, 29, 30, 68, 70
King's green, 29
King's Ride, 46
Kingsey near Haddenham, 63
Kingsgate, 60
Knoll, The, 2, 8, 11, 68
Knollis, Frances, 11
Knollis, Rev. James, 12
Knotty Green, 19, 20

Lancaster Rose, Bateman, 66
Lancaster Rose, Mrs, 66
Lane End (Penn), 5, 21, 24
Lane House, 21, 71
Lark Rise, 15
Last Judgement, 9
Laundry Cottages, 42, 48, 71
Laurels, The, 64
Lee, William, 24
Little Barn, 59
Little Hatch, 16
Little House, The, 33
Little Mead, 21
Little Ranters (Rarnters), 61
Little Shelter, 21
Listed Buildings, indicator, 3
Locally Listed buildings, indicator, 3
Lloyds Bank, 30
Lluelyn, Martin, 63
London County Council, 28
Long, Esther, 53
Long, Henry, 53
Long Pond, 8, 14, 71
Long, Thomas, 34
Lost Chord, The, 16
Lost Cottage, 42, 58
Loudwater: driveway from Rayners; 27; riots; 12
Lucas Industries, 57
Lunnon, John, 23
Lyndhurst, 37

Maclean, Donald, 9
Madryn, 49
Magnolia, 53
Manor House, 16
Maidenhead to High Wycombe Railway, 27
Marlins, 15
Maufe, Sir Edward, 8
Mayfields, 37
Marylebone Station, 6, 20
Meadows, The, 21
Merchants Yard, 34
Memorial trees, 58
Menday, James, 59
Methodist Chapel, 18